HISTORY OF THE CERT BASIC TRAINII

MW01115645

The Community Emergency Response Team (CERT) supported, locally implemented initiative that teaches themselves for hazards that may affect their communi... ....ains them in basic disaster response skills such as team organization, disaster medical operations, fire safety, and light search and rescue. Local CERT programs train and organize teams of volunteers to assist their families, neighbors, co-workers, and other community members during emergencies when professional responders may not be immediately available to provide assistance. Before, during, and after disasters, CERT volunteer teams perform basic response activities, including checking in on neighbors, distributing information to the public, supporting emergency operations centers, and helping to manage traffic and crowds. The ability for CERT volunteers to perform these activities frees up professional responders to focus their efforts on more complex, essential, and critical tasks. CERT volunteers also support their communities by organizing, promoting, and participating in emergency preparedness events, activities, and projects.

The Los Angeles Fire Department (LAFD) developed the CERT program after examining the civilian response to disasters in Mexico and Japan in 1985. The LAFD recognized that citizens are likely to be on their own during the early stages of disaster. Under these circumstances, family members, co-workers, and neighbors will often spontaneously come to the aid of each other. While untrained volunteers can be very effective in aiding others, their lack of training puts them at risk for injury or death. For example, during the response to the 1985 Mexico City earthquake that claimed more than 10,000 lives, untrained volunteers saved 700 lives, but unfortunately, 100 volunteers died in the process.

In response, the LAFD decided to develop and offer disaster response training to Los Angeles residents so that during and after future disasters volunteers would be able to assist in a safe, responsible, and effective manner. The LAFD piloted the first CERT training in 1986. In turn, other fire departments around the country, including communities where the major threat is hurricanes rather than earthquakes, adopted the LAFD's training model. Building on this development, the Federal Emergency Management Agency (FEMA) expanded the CERT materials in 1994 to make them applicable to all hazards and made the program available to communities nationwide. Since that time, thousands of dedicated trainers, organizations, and citizens have embraced the responsibility to learn new skills and become prepared to execute safe and effective emergency response capabilities.

The National CERT Program Office would like to thank the regional, state, and local partners and subject matter experts who contributed to the 2019 CERT Basic Training update.

A MODEL FOR COMMUNITY PREPAREDNESS

The CERT program is critical in the effort to engage everyone in the United States in making their communities safer, more prepared, and more resilient when incidents occur.

Community-based preparedness planning allows us all to prepare for and respond to anticipated disruptions and potential hazards following a disaster. As individuals, we can prepare our homes and families to cope during that critical period. Through pre-event planning, neighborhoods, and worksites can also work together to help reduce injuries, loss of lives, and property damage. Neighborhood preparedness will enhance the ability of individuals and communities to reduce their emergency needs and to manage their existing resources until professional assistance becomes available.

Studies of behavior following disasters have shown that groups working together in the disaster period perform more effectively if there has been prior planning and training for disaster response. These studies also show that organized grassroots efforts may be more successful if they are woven into the social and political fabric of the community—neighborhood associations, schools, workplaces, places of worship, and other existing organizations.

Effective response, therefore, requires comprehensive planning and coordination of all who will be involved—government, volunteer groups, private businesses, schools, and community organizations. With training and information, individuals and community groups can be prepared to serve as a crucial resource capable of performing many of the emergency functions needed in the immediate post-disaster period. The CERT program trains individuals to be assets to help communities prepare for effective disaster response.

When Disaster Strikes

The damage caused by natural disasters, such as earthquakes, hurricanes, tornadoes, and floods, or from manmade/technological events such as explosions or hazardous materials accidents can affect all aspects of a community, from government services to private enterprise to civic activities. These events:

- Severely restrict or overwhelm our response resources, communications, transportation, and utilities; and
- Leave many individuals and neighborhoods cut off from outside support.

Damaged roads and disrupted communications systems may restrict the access of emergency response agencies into critically affected areas. Thus, for the initial period immediately following a disaster—often up to three days or longer—individuals, households, and neighborhoods may need to rely on their own resources for:

- Food;
- Water; and
- Shelter.

Individual preparedness, planning, survival skills, and mutual aid within neighborhoods and worksites during this initial period are essential measures in managing the aftermath of a disaster. What you do today will have a critical impact on the quality of your survival and your ability to help others safely and effectively. You will be more resilient to a potentially disruptive event by learning about the likely hazards in your community and your community's plans and protocols, understanding hazard-specific protective actions and response skills, assembling important emergency supplies, and mitigating potential hazards in your home. Subsequently, you will be an important asset to your family, neighbors, and other members of your community.

How CERTS Operate

As each CERT is organized and trained in accordance with standard operating procedures developed by the sponsoring agency, members identify potential meeting locations or staging areas to be used in the event of a disaster.

The staging area is where the fire department and other services will interact with CERTs. Having a centralized contact point makes it possible to communicate damage assessments and allocate volunteer resources more effectively. This is true for all CERTs, whether active in a neighborhood, workplace, school, college/university campus, or other venue.

Damage from disasters may vary considerably from one location to another. In an actual disaster, communities will deploy CERTs as needs dictate. Volunteers should assess their own needs and the priorities of those in their immediate environment first.

CERT volunteers who do not encounter a need in their immediate area should then report to their staging area, and the first volunteer to arrive will become the initial Team Leader (TL) for the disaster response. The TL may pass leadership to someone else as other volunteers arrive. Volunteers who find themselves in a heavily impacted location should send runners to staging areas to get assistance from available resources. Volunteers may use ham radios or similar technologies to increase communication capabilities and coordination.

CERTs provide an effective first-response capability. Acting as individuals first, then as team members, trained CERT volunteers can fan-out within their assigned areas, extinguish small fires, turn off natural gas at damaged homes, perform light search and rescue, and render basic medical treatment. CERTs also act as effective "eyes and ears" for uniformed emergency responders. Trained volunteers also offer an important potential workforce to service organizations in non-hazardous functions such as shelter support, crowd control, and evacuation.

About the CERT Basic Training

If available, emergency services personnel are the best trained and equipped to handle emergencies. Following a catastrophic disaster, however, you and your community may be isolated for an extended period for a myriad of reasons, including the size of the area affected, inoperable communications systems, or unpassable roads.

CERT Basic Training prepares you to help yourself and help others in the event of a catastrophic disaster. Because emergency services personnel will not be able to help everyone immediately, you can make a difference by using your CERT training to save lives and protect property.

This training covers basic skills that are important to know in a disaster when emergency services are not available. With training and practice, and by working as a team, you will be able to protect yourself and maximize your capability to help for the greatest number of people after a disaster.

COURSE OVERVIEW AND OBJECTIVES

The CERT Basic Training provides individuals who complete this course with the basic skills required to respond to their community's immediate needs in the aftermath of a disaster, when emergency services are not immediately available. By working together, CERT volunteers can help save lives and protect property using the basic techniques in this course. The target audience for this course is individuals who desire the skills and knowledge required to prepare for and respond to a disaster.

Overall Course Objectives

Upon completing this course, the participants should be able to:

1. Take steps to prepare themselves, their families, and their communities for a disaster;
2. Describe the function and organization of a CERT program and the role CERTs serve in immediate disaster response;
3. Recognize life-threatening conditions and apply appropriate life-saving techniques, conduct patient head-to-toe assessments, employ basic treatment for injuries, and understand disaster medical operations;
4. Describe the post-disaster emotional environment and the steps that volunteers can take to relieve their own stressors and those of disaster survivors;
5. Identify and reduce potential fire hazards in their homes, workplaces, and neighborhoods and perform basic fire suppression strategies, resources, and safety measures;
6. Describe the most common techniques associated with light search and rescue operations including identifying planning and size-up requirements, searching a structure, debris removal, survivor extrication, and rescuer safety; and
7. Explain current terrorism trends and measures CERT volunteers can take to increase preparedness before and safety during a terrorism incident.

In addition to the overall course objectives listed above, each unit has specific objectives.

COURSE AGENDA

The agenda for this course is outlined below. Please note that some adjustments to the agenda may be required to allow discussion of hazards specific to a community and—depending on class size—to allow all participants to take part in the exercise portions of this course.

Unit	Topics
1	**Disaster Preparedness** • Unit Overview • Community Preparedness: Roles and Responsibilities • Hazards and Their Potential Impact • Home and Workplace Preparedness • Reducing the Impact of Hazards Through Mitigation • CERT Disaster Response • Additional Training for CERT Volunteers • Unit Summary
2	**CERT Organization** • Unit Overview • CERT Organization • CERT Mobilization • Documentation • Unit Summary
3	**Disaster Medical Operations — Part 1** • Unit Overview • Treating Life – Threating Conditions • Basic First Aid Care • Unit Summary
4	**Disaster Medical Operations — Part 2** • Unit Overview • Mass Casualty Incidents • Functions of Disaster Medical Operations • Establishing Medical Treatment Areas • Conducting Head-to-Toe Assessments • Public Health Considerations • Unit Summary
5	**Disaster Psychology** • Unit Overview • Disaster Reactions • Self-Care and Team Well-Being • Working with Survivors' Emotional Responses • Unit Summary

Unit	Topics
6	**Fire Safety and Utility Controls** • Unit Overview • Fire Chemistry • Fire Size-up Considerations • Firefighting Resources • Fire Suppression Safety • Fire and Utility Hazards • Hazardous Materials • Unit Summary
7	**Light Search and Rescue Operations** • Unit Overview • Safety During Search and Rescue Operations • Conducting Interior and Exterior Search Operations • Conducting Rescue Operations • Unit Summary
8	**CERT and Terrorism** • Unit Overview • Terrorist Goals and Tactics • Preparing Your Community • Active Shooter Situations • Until Help Arrives • Hazmat and CBRNE • Unit Summary
9	**Course Review, Final Exam, and Disaster Simulation** • Unit Overview • Course Review • Final Exam • Disaster Simulation • Exercise Critique and Summary

AFTER CERT BASIC TRAINING

Upon completion of the CERT Basic Training course, you will receive a certificate. Your community may also provide additional documents that will identify you as an emergency response team volunteer during disaster response.

In addition, you should maintain your CERT safety equipment—such as goggles, gloves, and basic first aid supplies—and have them available for use during a disaster. Training in disaster response should not be a one-time event. You should reinforce your skills through follow-up training and repeated practice to maintain the skills necessary for effective response to a disaster.

To maintain your skill level and continually improve performance, you and your team should participate in continuing supplemental training when offered in your area. Working through practice disaster scenarios with other teams will provide opportunities not only for extended practice, but also for valuable networking with teams in the local area.

CERT Unit 1: Disaster Preparedness

Participant Manual

CERT Basic Unit 1: Disaster Preparedness

In this unit, you will learn about:

☐ **Roles and Responsibilities for Community Preparedness:** How everyone in a community has a role in disaster preparedness.

☐ **Role of CERTs:** CERT organization, disaster and non-disaster roles, and laws that protect disaster workers from liability.

☐ **Elements of Disasters and Their Impact on Infrastructure:** The potential effects of extreme emergencies and disasters on electrical service; emergency services; telephone communication; transportation; and availability of food, water, shelter, and fuel.

☐ **Personal and Organizational Preparedness:** How you can prepare in advance to improve the quality of your survival and to reduce the damage from hazards.

CERT Unit 1 Table of Contents

SECTION 1: UNIT 1 OVERVIEW

Setting the Stage

The damage caused by natural disasters and manmade events can be extensive. While emergency services personnel are the best trained and equipped to handle emergencies, they may not be immediately available following a disaster. In such a situation, volunteers of the community may be on their own for several days or longer. They may have to rely on their own resources for food, water, first aid, and shelter. Additionally, neighbors or coworkers may have to provide immediate assistance to those who are hurt or need help.

Community Emergency Response Teams (CERTs) respond in the period immediately after a disaster when response resources are overwhelmed or delayed.

CERTs are able to:

- Assist emergency services personnel when requested in accordance with standard operating procedures (SOPs) developed by the sponsoring agency and by area of training;
- Assume some of the same functions as emergency services personnel following a disaster; and
- Prepare families and communities prior to emergencies and assist neighbors during an emergency when first responders are not immediately available.

While CERTs are a valuable asset in emergency response, CERTs are not trained to perform all of the functions to respond to the same degree as professional responders. CERTs are a bridge to professional responders until they are able to arrive. This training covers basic skills that are important to know in a disaster when emergency services personnel are not immediately available.

Unit 1 Objectives

At the end of this unit on disaster preparedness, you should be able to:

1. Describe the functions of CERT, discuss your role as CERT volunteers, and explain how CERT fits into your community's emergency preparedness structure;
2. Describe the types of hazards most likely to affect your communities and their potential impact on people, health, and infrastructure; and
3. Prepare yourself and your family for potential disasters your community may face, including learning to create a family disaster plan and emergency preparedness kit.

Exercise 1.1: Building a Tower

Instructions: Follow the steps below to complete this exercise:

1. Work in groups of five to design and construct a freestanding tower that stands at least 5 feet tall from the bottom of the structure to the top.
2. You will have a total of 10 minutes. Spend the first 5 minutes planning and designing the tower as a group. While you are planning, you should not touch any of the materials.
3. Wait to be instructed when to begin construction; you will have 5 minutes from that point to complete the tower.

The problem solving, communication, and team coordination skills that you use during this exercise are the same skills that you will use as CERT volunteers.

SECTION 2: COMMUNITY PREPAREDNESS ROLES AND RESPONSIBILITIES

Community preparedness is a key priority in lessening the impact of disasters. It is critical that all community members take steps to prepare in advance of an event. Effective community preparedness addresses the unique attributes of the community:

- The threat and hazards profile and vulnerabilities of the area;
- The existing infrastructure;
- Resources and skills within the community; and
- The population composition of the community.

Effective community preparedness also engages the whole community, which includes:

- Government leaders and the public sector;
- Community leaders from the private and civic sectors; and
- The public, including volunteer groups, faith-based groups, and tribal communities.

Government

Government has the responsibility to develop, test, and refine emergency operations plans; ensure emergency responders have adequate skills and resources; and provide services to protect and assist its citizens. In meeting these challenges, government also has the responsibility to involve the community in the planning process, to incorporate community resources in the plans, to provide reliable, actionable information, and to encourage training, practicing, and volunteer programs.

Government emergency service providers include professionals from the following fields:

- Emergency management;
- Emergency medical services;
- Fire and rescue;
- Human services;
- Law enforcement;
- Public health services; and
- Public works.

The Emergency Operations Plan (EOP)

All government agencies with a role in disaster response work to organize and coordinate their agencies' activities before an emergency or disaster. The product of their work is the Emergency Operations Plan (EOP) for that community.

The EOP is a document that:

- Assigns responsibility to organizations and individuals for carrying out specific actions at projected times and places in an emergency that exceeds the capability or routine responsibility of any one agency (e.g., the fire department);

- Sets forth lines of authority and organizational relationships and shows how all actions will be coordinated;
- Describes how to protect people and property in emergencies and disasters; and
- Identifies personnel, equipment, facilities, supplies, and other resources available—within the jurisdiction or by agreement with other jurisdictions—for use during response and recovery operations.

In short, the EOP describes how the community will function in an emergency.

Community Leaders

Community leaders from the private and civic sectors have a responsibility to participate in community preparedness. Their responsibilities include:

- Participating on the local collaborative planning council to provide insights and perspectives reflecting their industry or the constituency they service. For example, people with disabilities, local schools, communities with language or cultural differences, small businesses, the economically disadvantaged, and communities of faith;
- Identifying and integrating appropriate resources into government plans; and
- Ensuring facilities, staff, and customers or population served are prepared, trained, and practiced in preparedness actions.

The Public

The public also has a responsibility for preparedness. All members of the community should:

- Learn about the community alerts and warnings, evacuation routes, and how to get critical information;
- Take training in preparedness, first aid, and response skills;
- Practice skills and personal plans through periodic drills in multiple settings;
- Network and be able to help others;
- Participate in community feedback opportunities;
- Report suspicious activity; and
- Volunteer.

Engaging the Whole Community

FEMA's Whole Community approach to emergency management seeks to engage the full capacity of society in a dialogue to increase disaster preparedness and resilience. The full capacity of society is a reference to all of the partners within a community who should engage in community preparedness, including government entities; non-governmental organizations; faith-based organizations; schools; nonprofit groups; private sector entities; and at the grass roots level, individuals, families, local communities, and social networks.

Community coalitions organized collaborative bodies within a community such as Citizen Corps help to foster and strengthen relationships throughout the community. Relationships are the fabric that makes a community stronger and more resilient after disasters. *Social capital* is the value we place on our relationships with one another. Studies have shown that communities that possess a high amount of social capital bounce back much more efficiently after a disaster and tend to rely less on outside resources to return to normal.

Despite advances in technology, a functioning community is based on complex and interdependent systems driven by human forces. Community coalitions bring government and community leaders together to ensure emergency plans more effectively reflect the community's needs, challenges, capabilities, and resources.

Get Involved

Preparedness requires active participation from all. Below are some steps to get involved.

- Start the process by talking to your friends and family about the hazards in your area and discuss what steps—large or small—you all need to take to be able to help each other in a crisis.
- Ask about emergency planning at your workplace, schools, places of worship, and other social settings.
- Make sure those individuals in charge have a plan and are connected to community authorities on emergency management and planning.
- Take training to acquire the skills you need to help others and keep your skills current through refresher training and practice.
- Participate in the CERT program to provide training, practice, and the connection with others to develop teams.
- Plan to participate in drills and exercises with your family and neighbors and at your workplace, school, place of worship, and community-organized events. The more you practice, the better prepared you will be to take effective action when a disaster happens.
- Talk to your friends and family about volunteering. Volunteering to help your community through CERT and other activities is a great experience to share!

SECTION 3: HAZARDS AND THEIR POTENTIAL IMPACT

Types of Disasters

Disasters can be:

- Natural (e.g., earthquakes, wildfires, floods, extreme heat, hurricanes, landslides, thunderstorms, tornadoes, tsunamis, volcanic eruptions, winter storms);
- Technological and Accidental (e.g., hazardous material spill, nuclear power plant accident);
- Terrorism (chemical, biological, radiological, nuclear, or explosive weapons);
- Pandemics; and
- Home Fires.

CERT volunteers will generally respond to large-scale events in their communities. The scope of this CERT training does not cover pandemics. While home fires are not always community events, Unit 6: Fire Safety and Utility Controls, does discuss them. For the purposes of this training, most of the hazards discussed will be natural, technological and accidental, or terrorism related.

Key Elements of Disasters

Regardless of the event, disasters have several key elements in common.

- They are relatively unexpected, with the little or no warning or opportunity to prepare.
- Increased demands for resources may initially overwhelm available response personnel and emergency services.
- They endanger lives, health, and the environment.

In the immediate aftermath of a disaster, needs are often greater than professional emergency services personnel can provide. In these instances, CERTs become a vital link in the emergency service chain.

Understanding Local Hazard Vulnerability

Assessing your community's vulnerability to hazards allows the community to prioritize preparedness measures and to target effective actions for the appropriate hazard. To assess your community's vulnerability to hazards, it is useful to:
- Identify the most common disasters that occur;
- Identify possible hazards with most severe impact;
- Consider recent and/or historical impacts;
- Identify susceptible locations in the community for specific hazards—people, buildings, infrastructure; and
- Consider what to expect for disruption of services and length of restoration.

Impact on Infrastructure

Infrastructure and essential service providers that enable our communities to thrive and grow have become increasingly interconnected. Impacts in one area often affect essential government services, businesses, and individuals in an entire region with far-reaching health, safety, economic, and environmental consequences (see **Table 1.1**).

Table 1.1: Examples of Possible Impact on Infrastructure

Infrastructure at Risk	Possible Impacts
Transportation	• Roads are closed and/or impassable • Responders may be delayed in reaching areas of need • Flow of needed supplies (e.g., food, water) is interrupted
Structures	• Damaged critical facilities (e.g., hospitals, fire stations, police precincts, airports) unable to function • Increased risk of damage from falling debris
Communications Systems	• Survivors unable to phone for help or reach service providers • Coordination of services is hampered • Families and friends cannot communicate
Utilities	• Loss of service • Increased risk of fire or electrical shock • Limited access to fuel (e.g., pumps that may not work)
Water Service	• Medical facilities hampered • Inadequate water flow, which results in notice to boil water and hampered firefighting capabilities • Increased risk to public health
Fuel Supplies	• Increased risk of fire or explosion from fuel line rupture • Flow of fuel is interrupted by impassable roads
Financial Services	• ATMs do not work • Credit card systems inoperable

Consequences of Damage to Infrastructure

Each instance of damage to infrastructure may severely restrict the abilities of police, fire, and emergency medical services in that disaster. During a disaster, hospital emergency room personnel prioritize resources based on the severity of each injury. For emergency room personnel, life-threatening injuries take the highest priority and they treat them first. In the same way, during or after a disaster, emergency services personnel must prioritize resources according to the highest-priority need.

- Police will address incidents of grave public safety.
- Firefighters will suppress major fires.
- EMS personnel will handle life-threatening injuries. You should be aware, however, that CERTs may also handle life-threatening injuries until EMS units become available.
- Lower-priority needs will be met in other ways.

Damage Related to Structure Type

It is important to know what type of damage to expect from the main types of structures in the community. Engineered buildings, such as most high-rise buildings, have performed well in most types of disasters. During earthquakes, flooding events (e.g., hurricanes, tsunamis), and high-wind events (e.g., tornadoes, hurricanes), older high-rise buildings, however, are more susceptible to damage from:

- Broken glass;
- Falling panels; and
- Collapsing walkways and stairways.

Keep in mind that age, type of construction, and type of disaster are major factors in potential damage to detached homes and garages.

- Tornado and hurricane damage to single-family homes can range from little damage to total destruction.
- In general, homes built prior to 1940 were not originally bolted to the foundation, making them subject to being shaken, blown, or floated off their foundations.
- Older homes constructed of non-reinforced brick are less stable than newer construction.
- When an event damages a structure, there is a threat of additional damage, such as fire from ruptured gas lines, following the event.
- Mobile homes are most susceptible to damage because they can be displaced. When displacement occurs, structural integrity becomes questionable and utility connections may be damaged, increasing the risk of fire and electric shock.

In multiple-unit dwellings, there is often a main utility shutoff for the entire building, as well as a shutoff located within each individual unit. Depending on the situation at hand, you may need to use one or both. Be mindful of the effects and consequences of using each (Unit 6 will cover utility control in more depth).

Multiple-Use Buildings

Multiple-use buildings with oversized roof spans have a greater risk of collapse and broken glass in a disaster. These include:

- Airports;
- Malls and strip malls;
- Places of worship;
- Sports arenas; and
- Warehouse-type structures.

Non-Structural Hazards

There is also a risk in all types of structures from fixtures and other items within a home, garage, or workplace, that can pose a hazard during or after a disaster, including:

- Gas line ruptures from water heaters or ranges displaced by shaking, water, or wind;
- Damage from falling books, dishes, or other cabinet contents;
- Risk of injury or electric shock from displaced appliances and office equipment; and/or
- Fire from faulty wiring, overloaded plugs, frayed electrical cords.

Reducing hazards is an important part of personal preparedness. It is also important to know how and when to turn off utilities safely. Unit 6 – Fire Safety and Utility Control will cover utility shutoffs.

SECTION 4: HOME AND WORKPLACE PREPAREDNESS

FEMA is committed to social and physical science as the foundation for increasing individual and community preparedness. The agency has conducted national household surveys to assess the public's knowledge, attitudes, and behaviors on preparing for a range of hazards since 2007. The 2015 National Household Survey included key findings on individual preparedness, and in general, the preparedness concepts relayed throughout the CERT Basic Training.

- 68 percent of respondents reported having enough supplies to get through three days.
- 63 percent of respondents reported having taken steps to safeguard critical documents.
- 39 percent of respondents reported having sought preparedness information within the past year.
- 27 percent of respondents reported having talked to others about getting prepared within the past year.
- 18 percent of respondents reported having attended a preparedness meeting/training within the past year.

Preparing for a Disaster

Many preparedness actions are useful in any type of emergency, and some are specific to the type of disaster. A critical first step to preparedness is to understand the hazard or hazards that are most relevant to your community. Next, it is important to learn about local alerts and warning systems, evacuation routes, and sheltering plans. It is also important to familiarize yourself with hazards in other areas given that you may experience a different and less familiar type of hazard when you are traveling.

Regardless of the type of disaster, important elements of disaster preparedness include:

- Having the skills to evaluate the situation quickly and to take effective action to protect yourself;
- Having a family disaster plan and practicing the plan with drills;
- Assembling supplies in multiple locations;
- Reducing the impact of hazards through mitigation practices; and
- Getting involved by participating in training and volunteer programs.

It is always important to address specific needs, including any access or functional needs, considerations for pets and service animals, and transportation requirements for you and your family and friends. More information on preparedness is available online (see **Table 1.2**).

Websites of Interest

Table 2.2: Preparedness Websites

Organization	URL	Description
C.E.R.T. COMMUNITY EMERGENCY RESPONSE TEAM	https://www.ready.gov/community-emergency-response-team	Resources, trainings, and information about the CERT program.
Ready Prepare. Plan. Stay Informed.	www.ready/gov/	FEMA's national website for disaster preparedness. Provides excellent, general advice and is a good place to start.
Prepareathon	www.community.fema.gov	Prepareathon is a grassroots campaign to increase community preparedness and resilience.
American Red Cross	www.redcross.org	The American Red Cross website is full of excellent tips and information related to most of the natural disasters that occur, including a few topics not covered at FEMA's Ready.gov website.
CDC CENTERS FOR DISEASE CONTROL AND PREVENTION	www.pandemicflu.gov	The Centers for Disease Control and Prevention (CDC) established this website as a hub for national information on pandemic influenza.

Family Disaster Plan

In addition to knowing immediate protective actions that you may need to take, you should also create a family disaster plan. These plans can mean the difference between life and death in a disaster. Important considerations for your family disaster plan include:

- Where will you meet family members? You should have a location outside the house and another location outside the neighborhood;
- Identify an out-of-state "check-in contact;"
- Plan for all possibilities—extended stay, sheltering in place, or evacuation;
- How you will escape buildings where you spend time—your home, workplace, school, and place of worship; and
- What route (and several alternatives) will you use to evacuate?
- Do you have transportation?

Family safety is the most important factor when a disaster strikes. To make the most informed decision regarding your family's safety, you should first consider what option is best given the situation. It is also essential to practice your plan with your family—such as evacuating the home and contacting all family members using your "check-in contact." Practicing your plan now will improve your performance when it matters most.

Creating a Family Disaster Plan

To get started…

- Contact your local emergency management office and your local chapter of the American Red Cross.
    - Find out which disasters are most likely to happen in your community.
    - Ask how you would receive warnings about the event.
    - Find out how to prepare for each type of disaster.
- Meet with your family.
    - Discuss the types of disasters that could occur.
    - Explain how to prepare and respond.
    - Discuss what to do if advised to evacuate.
    - Practice what you have discussed.
- Plan how your family will stay in contact if separated by a disaster.
    - Pick two meeting places: 1) a location a safe distance from your home in case of fire and 2) a place outside your neighborhood in case you cannot return home.
    - Choose an out-of-state friend as a "check-in contact" for everyone to call.
        - Make sure the person selected understands that they are your out-of-state contact in case of emergency and what you would expect of them should such an emergency arise.
        - Give your "check-in contact" person a list of pertinent people to contact. Be sure to include phone numbers!
        - Periodically practice using your local and out-of-state contacts as if it were an emergency.
    - Prepare a business-card size list of family and friends' phone numbers and print one for each family member.
        - FEMA developed the Family Communications Plan to consolidate important contact information for emergencies. The two-page plan includes double-sided card printouts you can use for this purpose.
        - As a security measure, do not specify relationships.
- Complete the following steps:
    - Post emergency telephone numbers by every home phone and save in every cell phone.
    - Show responsible family members how and when to shut off water, gas, and electricity at main switches.
    - Install a smoke alarm on each level of your home, especially near bedrooms, and a carbon monoxide alarm in or near every bedroom. Test them monthly and change the batteries when you change your clocks in the spring and fall.

CERT Unit 1: Disaster Preparedness

- Contact your local fire department to learn about home fire hazards.
- Learn first aid and CPR.
    - Contact your local chapter of the American Red Cross, American Heart Association, or National Safety Council for information and training.
- Meet with your neighbors.
    - Plan how the neighborhood could work together after a disaster; know your neighbors' skills (e.g., medical, technical) and work with other community partners.
    - Consider how you could help neighbors, including the elderly or individuals who have access or functional needs.
    - Make plans for childcare in case parents cannot get home.

Assembling and Storing Disaster Supplies

You can cope best by preparing for a disaster before it strikes. One way to prepare is to assemble disaster supplies in multiple locations. After disaster strikes, you may not have time to shop or search for supplies. If you have gathered supplies in advance, you and your family can endure an evacuation or home confinement.

To Prepare Your Disaster Supply Kit

1. Review the checklists on the next few pages.
2. Gather the supplies from the list. Remember that many of the items needed for your kits are already in your household. It is possible to assemble these items in appropriate locations for quick access in an emergency but use under normal circumstances whenever needed. For example, keep a wrench in your kit to shut off gas at the meter in an emergency, but also use the wrench for everyday tasks. Just be sure to return it to the emergency kit.
3. Place the supplies you are likely to need for an evacuation in an easy-to-carry container. These supplies are listed with an asterisk (*).

Notes Regarding Your Disaster Supply Kit:

Water

- Store water in plastic containers such as soft drink bottles.
- Look for the triangular recycling symbol with a number 1 on the bottom of the bottle, as those are best for water storage. Avoid using containers that will degrade quickly or break, such as milk jugs or glass bottles.
- Wash the bottle with soap and warm water, fill with water from your tap, and store in a cool, dark area away from direct sunlight.
- Replace your emergency water every six months by repeating the process as all plastic degrades over time.
- Keep in mind that a normally active person needs to drink at least 2 quarts of water each day. Hot environments and intense physical activity can double that requirement. Children, nursing mothers, and ill people will need more.
- Store at least 1 gallon of water per person, per day (3 quarts for drinking, 1 quart for food preparation and sanitation).*

- Keep at least a 3-day supply of water for each person in your household.

If you have questions about the quality of the water, purify it before drinking. You can heat water to a rolling boil for 1 minute or use commercial purification tablets to purify the water. You can also use regular household liquid chlorine bleach if it is pure 5.25 – 6.0 percent sodium hypochlorite (see **Table 1.3**). (Do not use perfumed bleach!) After adding bleach, shake or stir the water container and let it stand 30 minutes before drinking.

Table 3.3: Ratios for Purifying Water with Bleach

Water Quantity	Bleach Added
1 quart	4 drops
1 gallon	8 drops
4 gallons	1/3 teaspoon

*Note: If water is cloudy, double the recommended amount of bleach.

Food and Kitchen Items

Store at least a 3-day supply of nonperishable food. Select foods that require no refrigeration, preparation, or cooking and little or no water. If you must heat food, pack a can of solid gel fuel. Select food items that are compact and lightweight. Avoid salty foods if possible as they increase thirst. **Table 1.4** includes a selection of foods to include in your disaster kit. Check expiration dates biannually.

First Aid Kit*

Assemble a first aid kit for your home and one for each car. (***Note:** This kit should not supplement or replace a CERT member supply kit!)

Special Items

Remember family members with special needs, such as infants and elderly or those with access and functional needs.

General

Supplies marked with an asterisk (*) can also be used for evacuation.

Table 4.4: Disaster Supply Items

Food Items	
• Ready-to-eat canned meats, fruits, and vegetables • Canned, juices, milk, soup (if powdered, store extra water) • Sugar, salt, pepper	• High-energy foods (Peanut butter, jelly, crackers, granola bars, trail mix) • Foods for infants, elderly persons, or persons on special diets • Comfort and stress foods (Cookies, hard candy, sweetened cereals, lollipops, instant coffee, tea bags)
Kitchen Items	
• Manual can opener • Mess kits or paper cups, plates, and plastic utensils • All-purpose knife • Small cooking stove and a can of cooking fuel	• Trash bags • Household liquid bleach to treat drinking water • Aluminum foil and plastic wrap
Disaster Kit First Aid Items	
• First aid manual • Two-inch sterile gauze pads (4-6) • Hypoallergenic adhesive tape • Needle • Antibacterial ointment • Tongue depressors (2) • Assorted sizes of safety pins • Non-latex exam gloves (2 pairs) • Four-inch sterile roller bandages (3 • rolls) • Sunscreen • Tweezers • Aspirin or non-aspirin pain reliever • Antacid (for upset stomach) • Laxative • Sterile adhesive bandages in assorted sizes	• Four-inch sterile gauze pads (4-6) • Triangular bandages (3) • Moistened towelettes • Thermometer • Tube of petroleum jelly or other lubricant • Cleaning agent/soap • Cotton balls • Three-inch sterile roller bandages (3 rolls) • Scissors • Hot and cold compress • Anti-diarrhea medication • Allergy medication and, if necessary, epinephrine • Activated charcoal

Disaster Kit Tools	
<ul><li>Emergency preparedness manual*</li><li>Battery-operated weather radio and extra batteries</li><li>Tube tent</li><li>Duct tape</li><li>Matches in a waterproof container</li><li>Plastic storage containers</li><li>Paper, pencil*</li><li>Work gloves</li><li>Flashlight and extra batteries*</li><li>Fuel for vehicle and generator</li><li>Plastic sheeting</li></ul>	<ul><li>Non-sparking shutoff wrench to turn off household gas and water</li><li>Pliers</li><li>Compass*</li><li>Fire extinguisher (small canister, ABC type)</li><li>Signal flare(s)*</li><li>Needles, thread</li><li>Medicine dropper</li><li>Whistle</li><li>Landline telephone</li></ul>
Personal Sanitation Items	
<ul><li>Toilet paper, towelettes*</li><li>Feminine supplies*</li><li>Household chlorine bleach</li><li>Disinfectant</li><li>Plastic garbage bags, ties</li></ul>	<ul><li>Soap, liquid detergent*</li><li>Personal hygiene items*</li><li>Plastic bucket with tight lid</li><li>Liquid hand sanitizer</li></ul>
Pet Items	
<ul><li>Medication and medical records (stored in a waterproof container)</li><li>Current photos of your pet in case they get lost</li><li>The name and number of your veterinarian in case you have to foster or board your pets</li><li>Sturdy leashes, harnesses, and/or carriers to transport pets safely and ensure that your animals can't escape</li></ul>	<ul><li>Food, potable water, bowls, cat litter, pan, can opener</li><li>Pet beds and toys, if easily transportable</li><li>Information on feeding schedules, medical conditions, and behavior problems</li><li>Pet first aid kit</li></ul>
Clothing and Bedding Supplies	
<ul><li>Sturdy shoes or boots*</li><li>Blankets or sleeping bags*</li><li>Thermal underwear</li><li>One complete change of clothing and footwear per person</li></ul>	<ul><li>Rain gear*</li><li>Hats and gloves*</li><li>Sunglasses*</li><li>Remember to cycle clothing for different seasons</li></ul>

Household Documents and Contact Numbers	
• Personal identification, cash (including change) or traveler's checks, and a credit card • Physical and electronic copies of important documents: birth certificates, marriage certificate, driver's license, Social Security cards, passports, wills, deeds, inventory of household goods, insurance papers, contracts, immunization records, bank and credit card account numbers, and stocks and bonds. Be sure to store these in a watertight and fireproof container • An extra set of car keys and house keys	• Emergency contact list and other important phone numbers • Map of the area and phone numbers of places you could go • Copies of prescriptions and/or original prescription bottles
Items for Infants	
• Formulas • Bottles • Medications	• Diapers • Powdered milk
For All Family Members	
• Heart and high blood pressure medication* • Other prescription drugs* • Contact lenses and supplies* • Entertainment (games, books)	• Insulin* • Denture needs* • Extra eye glasses*

Escape Planning

Develop an escape plan that provides for escape from every room of your home and every area of your workplace. As part of your escape plan you should:
- Consider the needs of children and individuals with access and functional needs;
- Inform all family members or office coworkers of the plan; and
- Run practice escape drills.

The following figure shows an example of an escape plan.

Image 1.1: Escape Plan

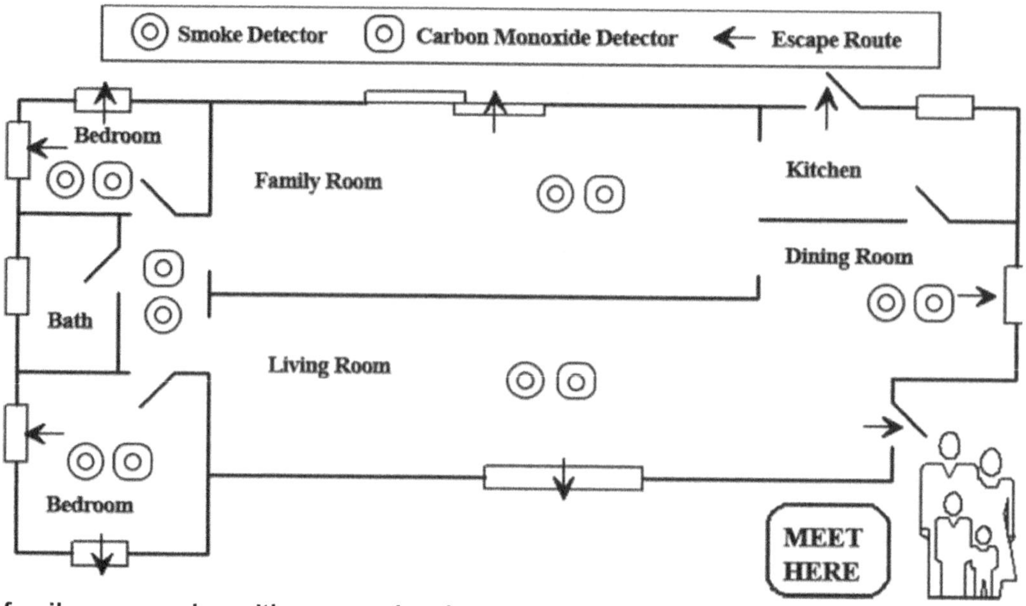

Sample family escape plan with arrows showing an escape route from every room in the home and a family meeting place outside the home

In most cases, homeowners will not have smoke alarms in every room, but it is important to have a smoke alarm at least on every level of the house. Practice your plans after you develop them. Conduct family fire drills, follow the local evacuation routes, and locate the nearest shelter to ensure that when a disaster occurs, you know what to do.

Exercise 1.2: Evacuate!

Instructions: Take the scenario given and decide what things to bring with you and/or what to do in the time available.

Protective Actions

Because many disasters occur with little or no warning, individuals need to have the knowledge and skills to take immediate protective actions in the first critical moments after a disaster has occurred—before you have instruction from authorities. While the specific actions to take are based on a number of variables (e.g., disaster type, amount of warning, amount of training you have taken, and location), the following list provides an overview of protective actions for which you should be familiar. These should be your objectives in assessing your post-event environment.

- **Assess the situation.** When something occurs without notice, it is important to take a few seconds to assess the situation to determine your most effective next steps, including identifying the type of event and determining whether the event has compromised air quality or a building structure.
- **Decide to stay or change locations.** In some instances, you should stay where you are (e.g., if you are inside and an event has occurred outside, you may need to stay inside) and in other circumstances you should change location (e.g., if

you are inside and the event is inside, you may need to evacuate the building). All disasters have unique attributes, so it is important for you to realize you may need to evaluate the circumstances to determine the best course of action

- **Staying or changing location is a critical early decision in disasters.** If you are not in immediate danger, you should stay where you are and get more information before taking your next steps. Thinking through the likely hazards in your community and where you might be when an event occurs may help you visualize your response. Additionally, consider your own circumstances and those of your household. Elderly persons or individuals with access and functional needs may need to evacuate well in advance of official notice or before the situation turns dangerous. While you may need to make the first immediate decision to stay inside or go outside or to shelter in place by sealing a room without authoritative instruction, it is important to listen to local authorities when they provide that information. If experts or local officials tell you to evacuate from your location, LEAVE!

- **Seek clean air and protect breathing passages.** Regardless of the type of disaster, clean air is a critical need. Actions to protect your breathing passages and to seek clean air may include covering your mouth with a cloth or mask, vacating the building, or sheltering in place by sealing an internal room while the airborne contaminant dissipates.

- **Protect yourself from debris and signal rescuers if trapped.** Protecting yourself from falling or precarious debris is an essential protective action. If trapped, protect your airways, bang on an object, or blow a whistle. Yelling should be a last resort.

- **Remove contaminants.** If contaminants are released into the area or you encounter liquid or solid contaminants, quickly remove contaminated clothing before washing yourself with soap and water, starting at the head and working toward the feet.

- **Practice good hygiene.** Good hygiene is a preventive measure for spreading disease, and it is important to be mindful of hygiene in a post disaster environment. Clean drinking water and sanitation are important protective actions.

Sheltering

There are different types of sheltering, and each are appropriate for different disasters.

- **Shelter in place:** Sealing a room is a way to protect yourself from contaminants in the air for a short period until the contaminants dissipate. You should identify an internal room in your home, at work, or other locations where you spend a great deal of time. If you are required to shelter in place, you will be in this room for only a few hours, but it is important that you be able to seal the room quickly. Storing specific items in the room is helpful. You should have snacks and water, a battery-operated radio, a flashlight, and pre-cut plastic sheeting and duct tape to seal off vents and door and window openings.

- **Shelter for extended stay:** Sheltering for an extended stay means you would stay where you are for several days or, in the case of a pandemic, authorities may ask you to limit your time outside the home for up to two weeks. It is important to store emergency supplies for these possibilities.

- **Mass care/community shelter:** These shelters often provide water, food, medicine, and basic sanitary facilities but, if possible, you should take your three-day disaster supplies kit with you so that you will be sure to have the supplies you require.

SECTION 5: REDUCING THE IMPACT OF HAZARDS THROUGH MITIGATION

Mitigation

Assembling disaster supplies and having a family disaster plan will help reduce the impact a disaster may have on you and your family. Mitigation is another approach you can take. Mitigation is the reduction of loss of life and property by lessening the impact of disasters. Mitigation includes any activities that prevent an emergency, reduce the likelihood of occurrence, or reduce the damaging effects of unavoidable hazards. A few examples include purchasing appropriate insurance and taking structural and nonstructural measures.

You should ensure your homeowner's policy provide adequate coverage and covers appropriate hazards for your area. Homeowner's insurance does not cover damage caused by flooding, so it is important to know whether you are in a flood hazard zone. If you are, it is strongly advised to purchase flood insurance. Visit the National Flood Insurance Program website, www.Floodsmart.gov, to learn more.

Some mitigation measures require a bigger investment to address structural changes to reduce the impact of disasters (see **Table 1.5**). Other non-structural mitigation measures may include relatively simple actions you can take to prevent home furnishings and appliances from causing damage or injuries during any event that might cause them to shift.

Table 5.5: Home Mitigation Measures

Type of Hazard	Sample Precautions
Structural	<ul><li>Bolt older houses to the foundation</li><li>Install trusses or hurricane straps to reinforce the roof</li><li>Strap propane tanks and chimneys</li><li>Strap mobile homes to their concrete pads</li><li>Raise utilities (above the level of flood risk)</li><li>Ask a professional to check the foundation, roof connectors, chimney, etc.</li></ul>
Non-Structural	<ul><li>Anchor furniture (e.g., bookshelves, hutches, grandfather clocks) to the wall</li><li>Secure appliances and office equipment in place with industrial strength hook and loop fasteners</li><li>Secure cabinet doors with childproof fasteners</li><li>Locate and label shutoffs for gas, electricity, and water before disasters occur. After a disaster, shut off the utilities as needed to prevent fires and other risks</li><li>Teach all home occupants, including children who are old enough to handle the responsibility, when and how to shut off the important utilities</li></ul>

Type of Hazard	Sample Precautions
	• Secure water heaters to the wall to safeguard against ruptured gas line or loose electrical wires • Install hurricane storm shutters to protect windows

Please note, a safe room is NOT the same as a shelter-in-place location. A safe room requires significant fortification for the room to provide protection against extremely high winds. More information regarding safe rooms is available at www.fema.gov/safe-rooms.

Sheltering-in-place protects you from contaminants in the air. To shelter in place, you do not need to alter the structure of the room. You are simply sealing the room with plastic sheeting and duct tape for a short time while the contaminants in the air dissipate.

Fortifying Your Home

Remember that different non-structural hazards pose different threats, depending on the disaster, as outlined by the following examples.

- Home Fires
    - Make sure that burglar bars and locks on outside window entries are easy to open from the inside.
- Landslides
    - Install flexible pipefittings to avoid gas or water leaks; flexible fittings are more resistant to breakage.
- Wildfires
    - Avoid using wooden shakes and shingles for roofing.
    - Clear all flammable vegetation at least 30 feet from the home.
    - Remove vines from the walls of the home.
    - Place propane tanks at least 30 feet from the home or other structures.
    - Stack firewood at least 30 feet away and uphill from the home.

For more information: "Learn About the Different Types of Disasters and Hazards" at www.fema.gov/hazard/index.shtm.

SECTION 6: CERT DISASTER RESPONSE

As described earlier in this unit, CERTs respond in the period immediately after a disaster when response resources are overwhelmed or delayed. CERTs assist emergency response personnel when requested in accordance with standard operating procedures developed by the sponsoring agency. Working as a team, members assume some of the same functions as emergency response personnel. As a reminder, while CERTs are a valuable asset in emergency response. CERTs are not trained to perform all of the functions or respond to the same degree as professional responders. CERTs are a bridge to professional responders until they arrive. CERTs respond after a disaster by:

- Treating life-threatening injuries until professional assistance is available;
- Helping disaster survivors cope with their emotional stressors;
- Locating and turning off utilities, if safe to do so;
- Extinguishing small fires; and
- Conducting light search and rescue operations.

There is a distinction between how a CERT volunteer responds to a disaster as an individual and how that volunteer responds as part of a team. In all instances, it is critical for CERT volunteers to stay within the limits of their training when providing disaster relief.

A CERT volunteer's first responsibility is personal and family safety. Only after CERT volunteers have secured their personal and family safety is it possible and pertinent to respond in a group capacity to do what is necessary for the community as a whole.

The sponsoring agency orchestrates its group response. In general, the team members select a leader (and alternate) and define the meeting location—or staging area—they will use in the event of disaster.

CERT volunteers gather at the pre-established staging area to organize and receive tasking assignments. Leaders may identify "runners" to serve as a communication link between the staging area and CERT volunteers working in the field.

In some cases, CERT volunteers also provide a well-trained workforce for such duties that entail shelter support, crowd and traffic management, and evacuation. It is important to note that when you become a CERT volunteer, you do not give up any rights you have as United States citizen. You can take the same legally permissible actions you would as an individual, but certain restrictions apply when acting as a CERT volunteer. When you put on the green CERT vest, you represent the agency or group that sponsored you.

CERT Organization

The chart below shows the basic CERT structure, including four sections. No matter which function CERT volunteers are assigned to, effective CERTs require teamwork.

There are checklists in the Additional Materials section at the back of Unit 1 in the Participant Manual that will help in:

- Planning and organizing a CERT; and
- Assembling equipment and supplies for a CERT.

CERT organization will be covered more in-depth in Unit 2: CERT Organization

Image 1.2: CERT Organization

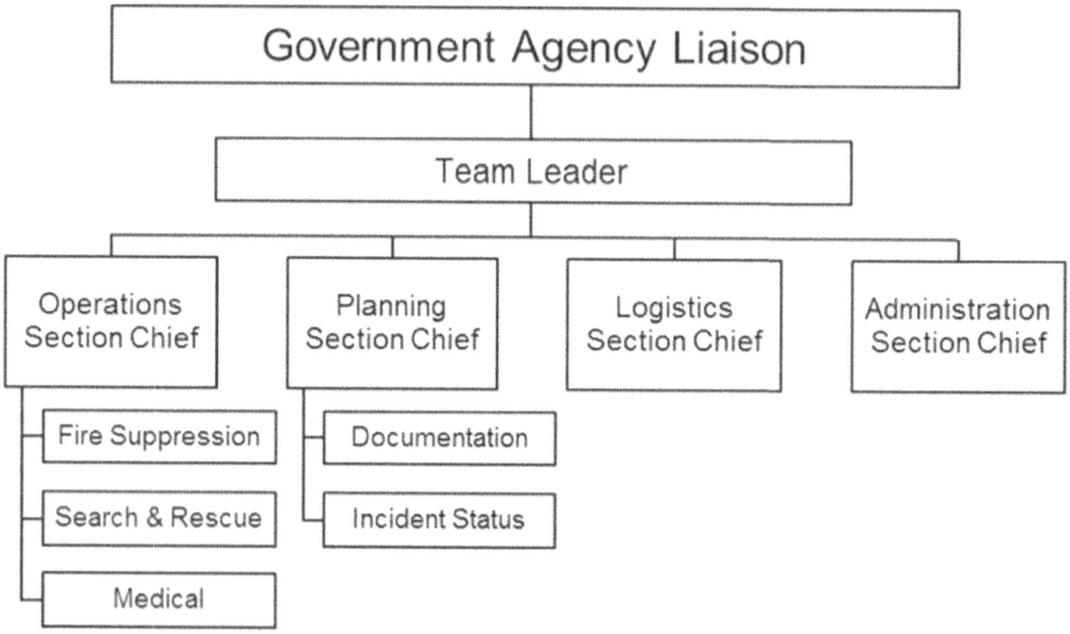

```
                    ┌──────────────────────────────────┐
                    │     Government Agency Liaison      │
                    └──────────────────────────────────┘
                                     │
                    ┌──────────────────────────────────┐
                    │            Team Leader             │
                    └──────────────────────────────────┘
          ┌───────────────┬──────────────┬──────────────┐
   ┌─────────────┐ ┌─────────────┐ ┌─────────────┐ ┌───────────────┐
   │ Operations  │ │  Planning   │ │  Logistics  │ │ Administration│
   │Section Chief│ │Section Chief│ │Section Chief│ │ Section Chief │
   └─────────────┘ └─────────────┘ └─────────────┘ └───────────────┘
      ├─ Fire Suppression     ├─ Documentation
      ├─ Search & Rescue      └─ Incident Status
      └─ Medical
```

- CERT organization showing the government agency liaison at the top.
- Underneath is the CERT Incident Commander/Team Leader who directs the activities of the four sections: Operations, Planning, Logistics, and Administration.
- Underneath the Operations section are three response teams: Fire Suppression, Search and Rescue, and Medical.
- Underneath the Planning section are two sections: Documentation and Incident Status.

Personal Protective Equipment

Remember that, at all times, <u>a CERT volunteer's first job is to stay safe</u>.

It is important to wear the appropriate personal protective equipment (PPE). CERT volunteers are required to wear the following:

- Helmet;
- Goggles;
- N95 Mask;
- Gloves (work and non-latex exam); and
- Sturdy shoes or boots.

CERT in Action

Across the country, CERTs continue to be activated in a wide range of disaster and emergency support operations. For these efforts, CERT volunteers and teams are receiving federal, state, and local recognition for their response assistance. For brief profiles on how CERTs have assisted in actual emergencies all over the country visit the national CERT website, <u>www.ready.gov/community-emergencyresponse-team</u>.

CERTs in Non-Disaster Roles

CERT volunteers are also a potential volunteer pool for the community. They can help with non-emergency projects such as:
- Identifying and aiding neighbors and coworkers who might need assistance during an emergency or disaster;
- Distributing preparedness materials and conducting preparedness demonstrations;
- Staffing first aid booths and preparedness displays at health fairs, county fairs, and other special events;
- Assisting with the installation of smoke alarms for seniors and special needs households; and
- Assisting with traffic and crowd management at large community events.

By participating in non-emergency community projects, CERT volunteers build recognition for the CERT program within their community and raise overall awareness of community preparedness. These events also provide CERT volunteers with valuable practice using the Incident Command System and operating with a partner.

Protection for Disaster Workers

"Good Samaritan" laws generally protect CERT volunteers who provide care <u>in a prudent and reasonable manner</u>.

The Volunteer Protection Act (VPA) of 1997 is a Federal law that protects volunteers from liability as long as they are acting in accordance with the training that they have received. VPA protects CERT volunteers during a disaster, and volunteers may also have further protection under relevant state statutes where they reside.

For additional information:
https://www.nonprofitrisk.org/app/uploads/2017/01/stateliability-laws.pdf

Table 1.6: Local Laws in Your Area

Applicable Laws and Key Points	
Applicable Laws	Key Points

SECTION 7: ADDITIONAL TRAINING FOR CERT VOLUNTEERS

After completing initial CERT training, many CERT volunteers seek to expand and improve their skills through continuing CERT modules offered locally, courses offered through the American Red Cross, or programs from other sources. Some CERT volunteers have sought additional training opportunities in:

- Advanced first aid;
- Animal issues in disasters;
- Automated External Defibrillator (AED) use;
- Community relations;
- CPR skills;
- Debris removal;
- Donations management;
- HAM radio;
- Shelter management;
- Special needs concerns;
- Traffic and crowd control; and
- Utilities control.

There are also Independent Study (IS) courses available online from FEMA that would be of interest to CERT volunteers. Some of these include:

- IS-100: Introduction to Incident Command System (ICS);
- IS-200: ICS for Single Resources and Initial Action Incidents;
- IS-700: National Incident Management System (NIMS), An Introduction; and
- IS-800: National Response Framework, An Introduction.

For a complete listing and access to FEMA IS courses, visit www.training.fema.gov/IS/. Click on the "IS Course List" link.

CERT Unit 1: Additional Materials

Additional Materials:

- [ ] CERT Team Organizational Checklist
- [ ] CERT PPE Checklist
- [ ] Recommended CERT Equipment and Supplies
- [ ] Disaster Preparedness Kit Checklist

CERT UNIT 1: ADDITIONAL MATERIALS

CERT Team Organizational Checklist

Instructions: This checklist will help guide you in the setup of your CERT program.

Table 6.7: CERT Team Organizational Checklist

Team Organization		Check of Complete	Date Completed
CERT Leadership	Team Leader	☐	
	Group Leaders	☐	
Membership	Roster	☐	
	Phone	☐	
	Phone List	☐	
	Skills Inventory	☐	
Communications	Telephone Tree	☐	
	Newsletter	☐	
	Amateur Radio	☐	
	Runners	☐	
Resources	Personnel	☐	
	Equipment	☐	
	Supplies	☐	
	Personal CERT Kit	☐	
Area Surveys and Locations	Evacuation Plans	☐	
	Staging Area/Command Post	☐	
	Medical Treatment Area	☐	
	Specific Hazard Areas	☐	
	Area Maps	☐	
Response Plan	Response Criteria	☐	
	Communications and Notifications	☐	
	Staging Area/Command Post	☐	
Teamwork	Meetings	☐	
	Drills and Exercises	☐	
	Training	☐	
	First Aid	☐	
	CPR	☐	
	Other	☐	

CERT PPE Checklist

Instructions: The following items are minimum safety equipment for all CERT volunteers.

Table 7.8: CERT PPE Checklist

PPE	Check if Obtained	Date Complete
Hard hat	☐	
Protective eyewear (safety goggles)	☐	
N-95 Mask	☐	
Long-sleeved shirt	☐	
Leather work gloves	☐	
Reflective vest	☐	
Long pants	☐	
Sturdy shoes or boots	☐	

Recommended CERT Equipment and Supplies

In addition to team supplies, the following equipment and supplies are recommended as minimum kit items for each CERT volunteer.

Table 8.9: Recommended CERT Equipment and Supplies

Equipment and Supplies	Check if Obtained	Quantity	Date Item Obtained
Nylon or canvas bag with shoulder strap	☐		
Water (two canteens or bottles per search and rescue team)	☐		
Dehydrated foods	☐		
Water purification tablets	☐		
Non-latex exam gloves (10 pair minimum)	☐		
Flashlight or miner's lamp	☐		
Secondary flashlight	☐		
Batteries and extra bulbs	☐		
Cyalume stick (12-hour omni glow)	☐		
Voltage tick meter	☐		
Pealess whistle	☐		
Utility knife	☐		
Notepads	☐		
Markers (thin and thick point)	☐		

Equipment and Supplies	Check if Obtained	Quantity	Date Item Obtained
Pens	☐		
Duct tape	☐		
Two-inch masking tape	☐		
Scissors (EMT shears)	☐		
Non-sparking crescent wrench	☐		
First aid pouch containing: ☐ 4-inch by 4-inch gauze dressings (6) ☐ Abdominal pads (4) ☐ Triangular bandages (4) ☐ Band-Aids ☐ Roller bandage ☐ Any personal medications that a CERT member may need during deployment.	☐		

Disaster Preparedness Kit Checklist

This checklist contains the full list of items recommended for your home disaster preparedness kit discussed within the unit. It is formatted as a checklist to assist in your planning purposes.

Table 9.10: Personal Disaster Kit Checklist

Category	Item	Check if Completed	Date Item Obtained
Food and Water	Water Stored in plastic containers	☐	
	Ready-to-eat canned meats, fruits, and vegetables	☐	
	Sugar, salt, pepper	☐	
	High-energy foods (peanut butter, jelly, crackers, granola bars, trail mix)	☐	
	Food for infants, elderly persons, or persons on special diets	☐	
	Comfort and stress foods (cookies, hard candy, sweetened cereals, lollipops instant coffee, tea bags)	☐	
Kitchen Items	Manual can opener	☐	
	Garbage bags	☐	
	Mess kits or paper cups, plates, and plastic utensils	☐	
	Household liquid bleach to treat drinking water	☐	
	All-purpose knife	☐	
	Aluminum foil and plastic wrap	☐	
	If food must be cooked, small cooking stove and a can of cooking fuel	☐	
First Aid	First aid manual	☐	
	Sterile adhesive bandages in assorted sizes	☐	
	Two-inch sterile gauze pads (4-6)	☐	
	Four-inch sterile gauze pads (4-6)	☐	
	Hypoallergenic adhesive tape	☐	
	Triangular bandages (3)	☐	
	Needle	☐	
	Moistened towelettes	☐	
	Antibacterial ointment	☐	
	Thermometer	☐	
	Tongue depressors (2)	☐	
	Tube of petroleum jelly or other lubricant	☐	
	Assorted sizes of safety pins	☐	

Category	Item	Check if Completed	Date Item Obtained
	Cleaning agent/soap	☐	
	Non-latex exam gloves (2 pairs)	☐	
	Cotton Balls	☐	
	Four-inch sterile roller bandages (3 rolls)	☐	
	Three-inch sterile roller bandages (3 rolls)	☐	
	Sunscreen	☐	
	Scissors	☐	
	Tweezers	☐	
	Hot and cold compress	☐	
Nonprescription Medication	Aspirin or non-aspirin pain reliever	☐	
	Anti-diarrhea medication	☐	
	Antacid (for upset stomach)	☐	
	Allergy medication, and if necessary, epinephrine	☐	
	Laxative	☐	
	Activated charcoal	☐	
	Emergency preparedness manual	☐	
	Battery-operated weather radio and extra batteries	☐	
	Flashlight and extra batteries	☐	
	Aluminum foil	☐	
	Tube tent	☐	
	Pliers	☐	
	Duct tape	☐	
	Compass	☐	
	Matches in a waterproof container	☐	
	Fire extinguisher (small containers, ABC type)	☐	
	Plastic storage containers	☐	
	Signal flares	☐	
	Paper, pencil	☐	
	Needles, thread	☐	
	Work gloves	☐	
	Medicine dropper	☐	
	Fuel for vehicle and generator	☐	
	Pealess whistle	☐	
	Plastic sheeting	☐	
	Landline telephone	☐	

Category	Item	Check if Completed	Date Item Obtained
	Non-sparking shutoff wrench to turn off household gas and water	☐	
Sanitation	Toilet paper towelettes	☐	
	Soap, liquid detergent	☐	
	Feminine supplies	☐	
	Personal hygiene items	☐	
	Plastic garbage bags, ties (for personal sanitation uses)	☐	
	Plastic bucket with tight lid	☐	
	Disinfectant	☐	
	Liquid hand sanitizer	☐	
	Household chlorine bleach	☐	
Clothing and Bedding	Sturdy shoes or boots	☐	
	Rain gear	☐	
	Blankets or sleeping bags	☐	
	Hat and gloves	☐	
	Thermal underwear	☐	
	Sunglasses	☐	
Household Documents and Information	Personal identification, cash (including change) or traveler's checks, and a credit card	☐	
	Physical and electronic copies of important documents: birth certificates, marriage certificate, driver's license, Social Security cards, passport, wills, deeds, inventory of household goods, insurance papers, contracts, immunization records, bank and credit card account numbers, stocks and bonds. Be sure to store these in a watertight and fireproof container.	☐	
	Emergency contact list and other important phone numbers	☐	
	Map of the area and phone numbers of places you could go	☐	
	An extra set of cat keys and house keys	☐	
	Copies of prescriptions and/or original prescription bottles	☐	

Category	Item	Check if Completed	Date Item Obtained
Items for Infants	Formula	☐	
	Diapers	☐	
	Bottles	☐	
	Powdered Milk	☐	
	Medications	☐	
Items for All Family Members	Heart and high blood pressure medication	☐	
	Insulin	☐	
	Other prescription drugs	☐	
	Denture needs	☐	
	Contact lenses and supplies	☐	
	Extra eye glasses	☐	
	Entertainment (games, books)	☐	

CERT Unit 2:
CERT Organization

Participant Manual

CERT Unit 2: CERT Organization

In this unit you will learn about:

- **CERT Organization:** How to organize and deploy CERT resources according to CERT organizational principles.

- **CERT Size-up:** How to conduct the continual data-gathering and evaluation process at the scene of a disaster or emergency.

- **Rescuer Safety:** How to protect your own safety and your buddy's during search and rescue.

- **Documentation:** Strategies for documenting situation and resource status.

CERT Unit 2 Table of Contents

SECTION 1: UNIT 2: OVERVIEW

Setting the Stage

This Unit will cover the Incident Command Structure (ICS) in depth and how it applies to CERT programs. It is recommended, although not required, that course participants have completed the IS-100 (Introduction to Incident Command System) and IS-700 (Introduction to National Incident Management System [NIMS]) courses prior to the start of this Unit.

Unit Objectives

At the end of this unit, you should be able to:

1. Describe the CERT organizational structure;
2. Explain the ICS and how CERT operates within this structure;
3. Describe the 9-step On-Scene size-up process; and
4. Describe how to use CERT standard documents.

SECTION 2: CERT ORGANIZATION

Principles of On-scene Management

CERT organization is based on the Incident Command System (ICS), which is a proven management system used by emergency responders. On-Scene management in a disaster situation follows these principles:

- Maintain the safety of disaster workers. The CERT Team Leader (TL) must continually prioritize response activities based on the team's capability and training. TLs also maintain the principle that rescuer safety is the number one concern. CERT functional leadership assigns activities and accounts for team volunteers. CERT volunteers work in the buddy system and respond based on their size-up of the situations that they encounter.
- Provide clear leadership and organizational structure by developing a chain of command and roles that are known by all team volunteers. Each CERT member has only one person that he or she takes direction from and responds to.
- Improve the effectiveness of rescue efforts. Disaster information is collected, and responses are prioritized based on rescuer safety and doing the greatest good for the greatest number according to the team's capabilities and training.

CERT Application of On-Scene Management

The specific CERT organizational structure and protocols provide:

- A well-defined management structure (e.g., leadership, functional areas, reporting chain, working in teams);
- A manageable span of control that provides for a desirable rescuer-to-supervisor ratio, optimum 5-to-1 with an acceptable spread of 2-to-7;
- Common terminology that contributes to effective communication and shared understanding;
- Effective communication among team volunteers and with professional responders, including the use of radios;
- Consolidated action plans that coordinate strategic goals, tactical objectives, and support activities;
- Comprehensive resource management that facilitates application of available resources to the incident in a timely manner; and
- Accountability.

Objectives for CERT On-Scene Management

In a disaster situation, the CERT TL:

- Identifies the scope of the incident (e.g., What is the problem?);
- Determines an overall strategy (e.g., What can we do, and how will we do it?);
- Deploys teams and resources (e.g., Who is going to do what?); and
- Documents actions and results.

The Need for Flexibility

Disasters create a dynamic, ever-changing environment. The CERT organizational framework is flexible so that it can expand or contract depending on the ongoing assessment priorities determined by the CERT Team Leader, people, and resources available. This expansion and contraction help ensure:

- Rescuer safety;
- Doing the greatest good for the greatest number;
- A manageable span of control; and
- Accountability of CERT volunteers.

Incident Command System

The ICS is the system used by emergency response agencies to manage emergency operations. When a CERT activates, it becomes part of that system. This section will explain the ICS format and detail how CERTs both operate within the ICS and organize themselves to replicate that of the ICS structure.

Basic ICS structure for a CERT is established by the person who arrives first on the scene. This person becomes the TL. Initially, the TL may handle all of the command positions of the ICS but, as the incident evolves, he or she may assign personnel as needed to the ICS Command Functions:

- Operations Section Chief;
- Intelligence/Investigations Section Chief;
- Planning Section Chief;
- Logistics Section Chief; and
- Finance/Administration Section Chief.

Through an effective ICS, all CERT volunteers report through a chain of command to the TL. The TL reports to the first fire or law enforcement official at their location and takes direction from that person until otherwise directed or until the CERT is relieved.

Image 2.1: ICS Command Function Organization Chart

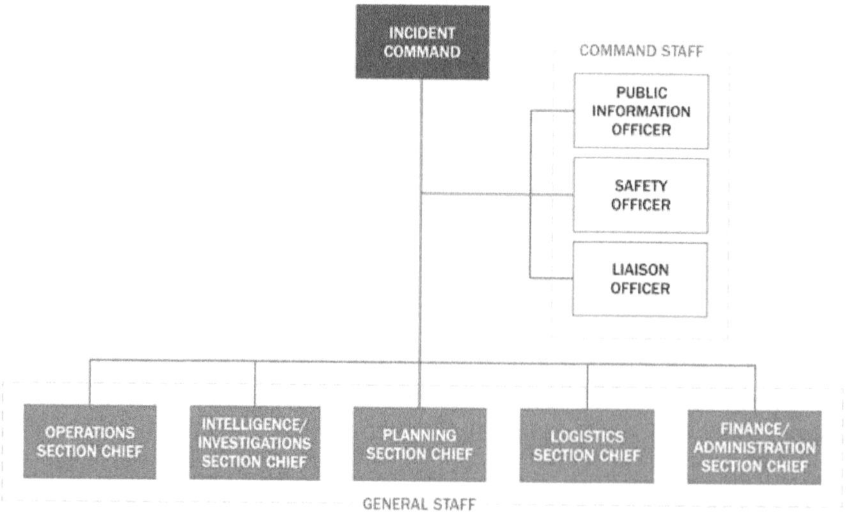

CERT Unit 2: CERT Organization   Participant Manual

Although there are a number of detailed responsibilities under each ICS function, the system itself is easy to understand. CERTs will typically require the Operations, Planning, and Logistics functions. The CERT Team Leader is responsible for handling or delegating each function to team volunteers.

As the incident expands, CERT volunteers are assigned or re-assigned to each section to handle specific aspects of the response while maintaining an effective span of control.

- CERT Team Leader:
  — Ensures incident safety;
  — Establishes incident objectives;
  — Delegates authority to others;
  — Provides information to internal and external parties;
  — Establishes and maintains liaison with other responders (e.g., fire, law enforcement, public works, other CERTs); and
  — Takes direction from agency officials.
- Intelligence/Investigations Section:
  — Prevents and deters potential unlawful activity, incidents, and/or attacks;
  — Collects, processes, analyzes, secures, and appropriately disseminates information and intelligence;
  — Conducts investigations; and
  — Informs and supports life safety operations.

Intelligence/Investigations is a function in the formal Incident Command System; however, CERTs will have a very limited involvement, if any, with this function.

- Planning Section:
  — Tracks resource status (e. g., number of CERT volunteers who have "reported for duty");
  — Tracks situation status;
  — Prepares the Team's action plan;
  — Develops alternative strategies; and
  — Provides documentation services.
- Logistics Section:
  — Provides communications;
  — Provides food and medical support to Team volunteers;
  — Manages supplies and facilities; and
  — Make sure that there are adequate resources (e.g., personnel, supplies, and equipment) for meeting the incident objectives.
- Finance and Administration Section:
  — Conducts contract negotiation and monitoring;
  — Keeps track of timekeeping;
  — Provides cost analysis; and
  — Tracks compensation for injury or damage to property.

Finance and Administration is a function in the formal Incident Command System; however, CERTs will have very limited involvement, if any, with this function.

CERT Operations

Based on the principles of ICS, CERTs follow these protocols:

- Each CERT must establish a command structure.
- The CERT TL directs team activities. During activation for a disaster, the first person at a pre-designated staging area assumes this responsibility. The initial TL may hand off this role to a pre-designated leader when that person arrives.
- The location established by the CERT TL as the central point for command and control of the incident is called the Command Post for the CERT. The TL stays in the Command Post. If the TL has to leave, the responsibility of TL must be delegated to someone in the Command Post.

Using the ICS structure, CERT volunteers are assigned to assist with a range of functions including:

- Logistics—managing resources, services, and supplies;
- Planning/Intelligence—collecting and displaying information; collecting and compiling documentation; and
- Operations—conducting fire suppression, medical operations, search and rescue.

In all situations, each unit assigned must have an identified leader to supervise tasks being performed, to account for team volunteers, and to report information to his or her designated leader.

In all situations, a manageable span of control is five rescuers per supervisor, with an acceptable spread of two to seven.

CERT personnel assigned to Operations should always be assigned to teams consisting of between one and five people:

- One person will serve as runner and communicate with the Command Post.
- Two people will "buddy up" to respond to the immediate needs.
- Search and rescue teams must include at least four people, with a safety team remaining outside the area subject to search, and at least two people to conduct the search.

Image 2.2: Expanded CERT Operations Structure

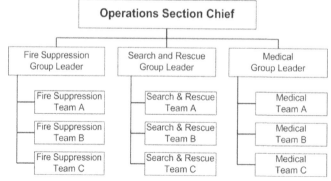

CERT operations section structure, showing the Operations Section Chief at the top and the three Group. Leaders underneath.

Dealing with the Media

CERT volunteers should refer any media inquiries to the CERT TL. The TL should then refer the media inquiries to the Public Information Officer of the CERT's sponsoring organization.

If the Public Information Officer of the sponsoring organization refers media to the CERT TL or otherwise authorizes them to speak with the media, the TL should:

- Refrain from addressing the media until doing so will no longer inhibit or delay the team's ability to do the greatest good for the greatest number in the shortest amount of time;
- Establish an area for briefing the media if necessary;
- Be careful about the information he or she releases, making sure it is both accurate and approved for release, while also keeping in mind victims' right to privacy; and
- Not feel compelled to answer every question asked.

National Incident Management System Implementation

The ICS is part of the National Incident Management System (NIMS). NIMS provides a consistent, comprehensive approach to incident management. It applies at all jurisdictional levels and across all emergency management functions and types of incidents.

NIMS was established so that first responders, including CERT volunteers, from different jurisdictions and disciplines can work together better to respond to disasters and emergencies.

- To meet NIMS standards, CERT volunteers must complete both the IS-100 (Introduction to Incident Command System) and IS-700 (Introduction to National Incident Management System [NIMS]) courses.
- Both independent study courses are available online from FEMA at http://training.fema.gov/IS/NIMS.asp.

Exercise 2.1: ICS Functions

Purpose: This activity will give you an opportunity to relate the ICS functions to specific situations.

Instructions:

1. Break into small table groups.
2. This exercise provides you with the opportunity to decide under which ICS functions the listed activities will fall.
3. Review the list of activities and use the initials, "TL," "O," "P," or "L" to indicate which ICS function would cover each activity.

While Finance and Administration is a part of ICS, it is generally not used by CERTs.

Using your knowledge about ICS functions, decide under which function the following CERT activities would fall. Some activities may involve more than one function to be completed (see **Table 2.1**).

Use the following key to fill in the blanks before each activity:

- Team Leader = TL;
- Operations = O;
- Planning = P; and
- Logistics = L.

Table 2.10: ICS Activities

Scenario	ICS Function
1. It's dark, all the lights are out, and you need additional flashlights to continue your response	
2. The designated first aid site has a downed power line.	
3. A neighbor reports the smell of gas in his house, but he cannot shut off the gas at the meter.	
4. The batteries for the portable radio are dead.	
5. The city wants to know the overall status of your neighborhood.	
6. Several of your neighbors have minor injuries and need first aid.	
7. Fire from another neighborhood is moving toward your neighborhood.	
8. There is a dog seen wandering near the first aid station.	
9. A news crew has arrived with a camera to film your activities.	
10. Two hysterical neighbors are demanding help. One cannot find her adolescent child who was playing outside when the disaster struck. The other wants help moving a bookcase off his wife. He says she's bleeding from a wound on the head.	
11. It's starting to rain. Your command post and the first aid area are not under shelter	
12. Too many people are coming to the Team Leader to ask questions. The Team Leader asks for someone to act as a "gatekeeper."	
13. There is a great increase of car and foot traffic through your neighborhood because other roadways are blocked.	
14. The Team Leader is very tired and is going to hand over responsibilities to someone else. He or she wants a report on the status of the neighborhood before doing so.	
15. Many neighborhood residents have come to volunteer their help.	
16. Reports have come in of damage and injuries in the next block. Teams must be assigned to assess the situation.	
17. A professional responder has arrived at the scene and would like a briefing on situation status.	

SECTION 3: CERT MOBILIZATION

The following steps describe how CERTs mobilize when an incident occurs:

- If the standard operating procedure (SOP) calls for self-activation, CERT volunteers proceed to the predesignated staging area with their disaster supplies. Along the way, they make damage assessments that would be helpful for the CERT TL's decision-making.
- The first CERT member at the staging area becomes the initial TL for the response. As other CERT volunteers arrive, the CERT TL may pass leadership to someone else. The CERT TL establishes operations to ensure effective communication, to maintain span of control, maintain accountability, and help the greatest number without placing CERT volunteers in harm's way.
- One of the CERT TL's first decisions will be to locate the team's Command Post. The staging area may become the Command Post; however, if another location would be safer or otherwise better, the Command Post should be set up there.
- As intelligence is collected and assessed, the TL must prioritize actions and work with the Section Chiefs or leaders. The CERT organization is flexible and evolves based on new information.

Following an incident, information—and, therefore, priorities—may be change rapidly. Communication between the CERT TL and response teams ensures that CERTs do not overextend their resources or supplies.

CERT On-Scene Size-up

On-Scene Size-up should be conducted upon CERT mobilization. Size-up is a continual process that enables professional responders to make decisions and respond appropriately in the areas of greatest need. CERT size-up consists of 9 steps and should be used in any emergency situation.

Refer the participants to CERT On-Scene Size-up in the Participant Manual. Although the checklist is not exhaustive, it does include many of the questions that CERT volunteers should ask when sizing up an emergency situation.

CERT Size-up Steps

The 9 steps of CERT size-up are:

1. **Gather facts.** What has happened? How many people appear to be involved? What is the current situation?
2. **Assess and communicate the damage.** Try to determine what has happened, what is happening now, and how bad things can really get.
3. **Consider probabilities.** What is likely to happen? What could happen through cascading events?
4. **Assess your own situation.** Are you in immediate danger? Have you been trained to handle the situation? Do you have the equipment that you need?
5. **Establish priorities.** Are lives at risk? Can you help? Remember, life safety is the first priority!

6. **Make decisions.** Base your decisions on the answers to Steps 1 through 5 and in accordance with the priorities that you established.
7. **Develop a plan of action.** Develop a plan that will help you accomplish your priorities. Simple plans may be verbal, but more complex plans should always be written.
8. **Take action.** Execute your plan, documenting deviations and status changes so that you can report the situation accurately to first responders.
9. **Evaluate progress.** At intervals, evaluate your progress in accomplishing the objectives in the plan of action to determine what is working and what changes you may have to make to stabilize the situation.

Table 2.2: CERT On-Scene Size-up Worksheet

Step 1: Gather Facts		
Time		
Does the time of day or week affect response efforts? How?	Yes	No
Weather		
Are there weather conditions that affect your safety? If yes, how will your safety be affected?	Yes	No
Will weather conditions affect the situation? If yes, how will the situation be affected?	Yes	No
Type of Construction		
What type(s) of structure(s) is (are) involved?		
What type(s) of construction is (are) involved?		
Occupancy		
Are the structures occupied? If yes, how many people are likely to be affected?	Yes	No
Are there special considerations (e.g. children, elderly, pets, people with access and functional needs)?	Yes	No
Hazards		
Are hazardous materials evident?	Yes	No
Are any other types of hazards involved? If yes, what other hazards?	Yes	No
Step 2: Assess and Communicate the Damage		
Survey all sides of the scene. Is the danger beyond the CERT's capability?	Yes	No
Have the facts and the initial damage assessment been communicated to the appropriate person(s)?	Yes	No

Step 3: Consider Possibilities		
Life Hazards		
Are there potentially life-threatening hazards? If yes, what are the hazards?	Yes	No
Additional Damage		
Is there a high potential for more disaster activity that will impact personal safety? If yes, what are the known risks?	Yes	No
Step 4: Assess Your Own Situation		
What equipment is available to support response efforts?		
What other resources are available?		
Can response be safely attempted by CERT volunteers? *If not, do not attempt response activities.*	Yes	No
Step 5: Establish Priorities		
Are there any other more pressing needs now? If yes, list.	Yes	No
Step 6: Make Decisions		
Where will resources do the most good while maintaining an adequate margin of safety?		
Step 7: Develop Plan of Action		
Determine how personnel and other resources should be used.		
Step 8: Take Action		
Put the plan into effect.		
Step 9: Evaluate Progress		
Continually size up the situation to identify changes in the scope of the problem, safety risks, and resources availability.		
Adjust strategies as required.		

Rescuer Safety

Effective emergency scene management requires the formulation and communication of strategic goals and tactical objectives to do the most good for the greatest number while maintaining the safety of rescue personnel.

Remember that **rescuer safety is paramount.**

The first question to ask is, "Is it safe for the CERT volunteers to attempt the rescue?" The answer to this question is based on the degree of damage:

- If the damage is heavy: No rescue should be attempted. Use tape around the area or mark the area as heavy damage. CERT volunteers do not have any legal authority to stop or restrict someone who wants to enter an area. At best, CERT volunteers can warn others about the danger and inform the CERT TL immediately if it is known that people are in the building.
- If the damage is moderate: Locate, assess (e.g., quickly evaluate and treat for airway obstruction, bleeding, and low body temperature), and immediately evacuate survivors to a safe area while minimizing both the number of rescuers inside the building and the amount of time that they remain inside.
- If the damage is light: Locate, assess, continue size-up, and document.

Table 2.3: CERT Rescue Efforts Based on Degree of Damage

Degree of Damage	Should Rescue be Attempted
Heavy	No, it is too dangerous to enter. Warn people to stay away. Inform the CERT TL immediately if it is known that people are in the building.
Moderate	Yes, but perform only quick and safe removals; limit onsite medical care to checking for breathing, stopping major bleeding, and maintaining body temperature. Minimize the number of rescuers inside the building.
Light	Yes, locate, assess, continue size-up, and document.

Image 2.3: CERT Tasks Based on Damage Level

Light Damage Site

Fire	Search & Rescue	Medical (on site)	Medical (off site)
- Shut off utilities as needed - Extinguish small fires - Document	- Locate - Assess - Treat airway/major bleeding - Continue sizeup - Document	- Assess again - Move to treatment area - Head-to-toe assessment - Treatment - Facilitate transport as needed - Document	- Assess again - Head-to-toe assessment - Treatment - Facilitate transport as needed - Document

Moderate Damage Site

Fire	Search & Rescue	Medical (on site)	Medical (off site)
- Shut off utilities if safe - Extinguish small fires - Document	- Locate - Assess - Treat airway/major bleeding - Evacuate - Warn others - Continue sizeup - Document	- Assess again - Move to treatment area (nearby safe location) - Head-to-toe assessment - Treatment - Facilitate transport as needed - Document	- Assess again - Head-to-toe assessment - Treatment - Facilitate transport as needed - Document

Heavy Damage Site

Fire	Search & Rescue
- Shut off utilities if safe - Document	- Mark area for heavy damage - Warn others - Gather information - Inform CERT TL immediately - Document

Tasks required of Fire, Search and Rescue, Medical, and Treatment Area teams based on the degree of damage to the structure.

SECTION 4: DOCUMENTATION

It is extremely important to document and communicate information about the disaster situation and resource status.

The efficient flow of information makes it possible for resources to be deployed effectively and for professional emergency services to be applied appropriately.

Documenting serves several purposes:

- The CERT TL will know what is happening throughout the incident.
- The CERT TL will have written information to pass on to the professional responders when they arrive.
- Communication improvement between functional areas and shifts.
- The CERT will be able to show how many volunteer hours it provided to the sponsoring agency or entity.
- Liability exposure will be documented.

Under the CERT structure, each level of organization has documentation responsibilities:

- Section Chiefs are responsible for providing the Command Post with ongoing information about damage assessment, group status, and ongoing needs.
- The Command Post is responsible for documenting the situation status, including:
  - Incident locations;
  - Access routes;
  - Identified hazards; and
  - Support locations.

Support locations include:

- A staging area;
- A medical treatment and assessment area; and
- A morgue, if there are fatalities.

This information is vital for tracking the overall situation and for the CERT TL to be ready to provide the documentation to the first professional responders on the scene.

Write it down! The most important thing to do is to write down what happened.

The information can be written down on the sample forms provided in this unit or it can be written down on sheet of paper.

Every entity, such as a functional team or staging location, must have a scribe to record everything. Typically, the CERT TL designates the scribe and provides some simple instructions.

Documentation Flow

Here is how a CERT would use these standard documents within the context of an event. Remind participants that, even if the forms are not used, this should give them an idea of the preferred information that needs to be collected and communicated between groups.

- CERT volunteers complete the Damage Assessment Form as they travel through the area to the CERT's staging location. The form is then given to the CERT TL. The form provides a summary of overall hazards in selected areas, and the information is used for prioritizing and formulating activities.
- The CERT TL assembles teams and makes assignments based on the damage assessment information. This person keeps the CERT Assignment Tracking Log, which is the most important tool for recording the activities of the functional teams and overall situation status.
- A scribe at the staging location signs in each volunteer using the Personnel Resources Check-In Form, noting any preferred team assignments or skills. This information needs to be passed on to the Command Post.
- The Command Post and the functional team share the Briefing Assignment Form. The CERT TL uses the front side of the form to communicate instructions (e.g., address, incident type, and team objectives) about the incident. The scribe of the functional team uses the blank side of the form to log team actions. The form is then returned to the Command Post when the team checks in.
- The Treatment Area Record is available to document each person brought into the treatment area and his or her condition.
- The Communications Log is on-hand to log incoming and outgoing transmissions; it is typically kept by the radio operator.
- The Equipment Inventory is kept in the area or vehicle in which equipment is stored.
- The General Message form is accessible for sending messages between any command levels and groups. The messages must be clear and concise.

Form 2.1: CERT Damage Assessment Form

DAMAGE ASSESSMENT FORM	CERT WILSONVILLE	DATE ## / ## / ##
LOCATION SE CORNER 16TH AND OAK ROAD UP TO THE SCHOOL IS CLEAR.		
CERT MEMBER SUSAN ADAMS		PAGE __1__ OF __1__

CERT FORM #1

Form 2.2: CERT Personnel Resources Check-In Form

CHECK IN TIME	CHECK OUT TIME	NAME	ID # (CERT badge or other)	CONTACT (cell # or radio)	PREFFERRED ASSIGNMENT FIRE	PREFFERRED ASSIGNMENT MEDICAL	PREFFERRED ASSIGNMENT SAR	SKILLS	TEAM ASSIGNMENT	TIME ASSIGNED
9:20 AM	12:45 PM	MARIANNE SHAW	756	(212) 522-2222				RADIO OPS	SAR 1	9:37 AM

PERSONNEL RESOURCES CHECK-IN

CERT WILSONVILLE

DATE ## / ## / ##

PAGE 1 OF 2

SCRIBE(S) JOHN TAYLOR, SHEILA EVANS

CERT FORM #2

Form 2.3: CERT Assignment Tracking Log

ASSIGNMENT TRACKING LOG

CERT: WILSONVILLE   DATE: ## / ## / ##

Assignment 1

ASSIGNMENT	Structural damage–Tornado
LOCATION	SE Corner 16th and Oak
TEAM	SAR 1
TEAM LEADER/CONTACT #	Marianne Shaw (212) 522-2222
START TIME	9:37 AM
END TIME	10:22 AM

Team members:
1. Tae Jin Kim
2. Kira Jah
3. Burt Manning
4. Alison McKittredge
5.

OBJECTIVES: To conduct a search and rescue of damaged high school gym.

RESULTS: No victims located. Gym lightly damaged. Saw heavy damage to west wing of school.

Assignment 2

ASSIGNMENT	
LOCATION	
TEAM	
TEAM LEADER/CONTACT #	
START TIME	
END TIME	

Team members:
1.
2.
3.
4.
5.

OBJECTIVES:

RESULTS:

Assignment 3

ASSIGNMENT	
LOCATION	
TEAM	
TEAM LEADER/CONTACT #	
START TIME	
END TIME	

Team members:
1.
2.
3.
4.
5.

OBJECTIVES:

RESULTS:

CERT LEADER/ INCIDENT COMMANDER: Elizabeth King

SCRIBE(S): Billy Rogers, Jorge Garcia

PAGE 1 OF 2

CERT FORM #3

Form 2.4a: CERT Briefing Assignment Form

BRIEFING ASSIGNMENT	CERT WILSONVILLE	DATE ## / ## / ##	
COMMAND POST CONTACT # (212) 555-1212		TIME OUT 9:50 AM	TIME BACK 10:36 AM

INSTRUCTIONS TO TEAM

TEAM NAME	LOCATION
Medical 2	Delmonico's Italian Restaurant, 810 King Street

OBJECTIVES

To conduct medical sizeup of any victims found.

EQUIPMENT ALLOCATED

REPORT FROM RESPONSE TEAM

FIRES		HAZARDS				STRUCTURE		PEOPLE			ROADS		ANIMALS		
BURNING	OUT	GAS LEAK	H20 LEAK	ELECTRIC	CHEMICAL	DAMAGED	COLLAPSED	INJURED	TRAPPED	DEAD	ACCESS	NO ACCESS	INJURED	TRAPPED	ROAMING
								3			✓				

CERT FORM #4 a

Form 2.4b: CERT Team Action Log

TEAM ACTION LOG
(time stamp each action; draw map if needed)

10:52 Team arrived at the restaurant. Made our way through the debris to victim #1, Bill Baker. Conscious and in pain. Ankle was trapped under a heavy bookcase. Extricated him. Two team members carried him to treatment area.

10:54 Victim #2, Carol Loughney. Bleeding on head from falling ceiling. Walked her to treatment area.

10:55 Victim #3. Found in kitchen. Unconscious but breathing. May have broken leg. Splinted leg. Moved by stretcher to treatment area.

SCRIBE
　　　Sam Ariton

CERT FORM #4 b

Form 2.5: CERT Treatment Area Record

VICTIM TREATMENT AREA RECORD

CERT: WILSONVILLE

DATE: ## / ## / ##

TREATMENT AREA LOCATION: RIDGEWAY PARK

TIME IN	NAME OR DESCRIPTION	CONDITION/TREATMENT (update as needed)	MOVED TO	TIME OUT
10:24 AM	Stephen Edmundson, 35 y.o. very tall	10:30 Heavy bleeding from cut at right temple—bandaged 10:45 Complained of dizziness and nausea	Sibley Hospital	12:15 PM

SCRIBE(S): REGGIE OSBORN

PAGE 2 OF 2

CERT FORM #5

Form 2.6: CERT Communications Log

COMMUNICATIONS LOG	CERT		DATE
	RADIO OPERATOR NAME		

LOG

TIME	FROM	TO	MESSAGE

PAGE_____ OF_____

CERT FORM #6 (Based on ICS 309)

Form 2.7: CERT Equipment Inventory Form

EQUIPMENT INVENTORY

CERT: WILSONVILLE DATE: ## / ## / ## PAGE 1 OF 1

ASSET #	ITEM DESCRIPTION	OWNER	ISSUED TO		QTY	TIME	INITIALS	COMMENTS
727820	STRETCHER	FD	MED 2	ISSUED	1	10:45 AM	AR	
				RETURNED	1	3:10 PM	AR	
				ISSUED				
				RETURNED				
				ISSUED				
				RETURNED				
				ISSUED				
				RETURNED				
				ISSUED				
				RETURNED				
				ISSUED				
				RETURNED				
				ISSUED				
				RETURNED				
				ISSUED				
				RETURNED				
				ISSUED				
				RETURNED				
				ISSUED				
				RETURNED				

SCRIBE(S): SYLVIE D'ANJOU

CERT Form #7 (Based on ICS 303)

Form 2.8: CERT General Message Form

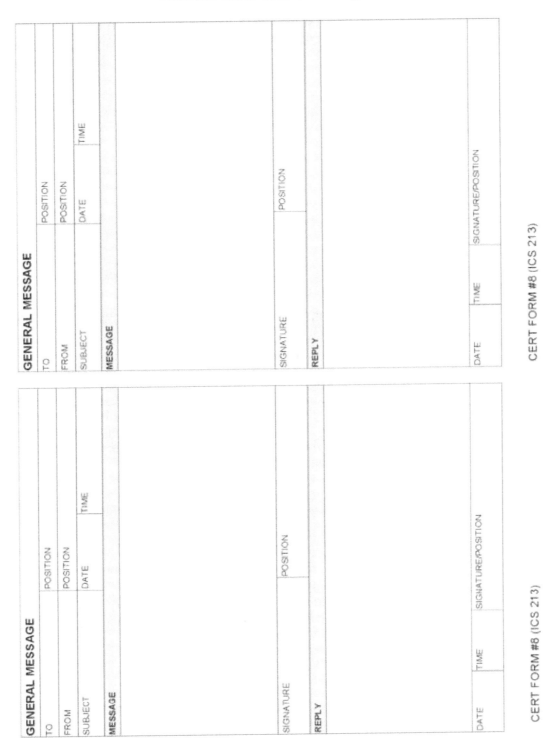

Documentation Forms

There are standard forms that can be used to facilitate documentation and information flow. The forms are functionally consistent with ICS forms and are designed to be NIMS compliant.

The CERT forms are:

- Damage Assessment;
- Personnel Resources Check-In;
- CERT Assignment Tracking Log;
- Briefing Assignment;
- Treatment Area Record;
- Communications Log;
- Equipment Inventory; and
- General Message.

Remember scribes can produce useful, high-quality documentation without using the forms as long as they take detailed notes of all activities.

Area maps, site maps, and building plans are also very useful for tracking response activities.

Table 2.4: Forms Used for Response Documentation

Form	Purpose
Damage Assessment [CERT Form #1]	Completed by CERT volunteers as they travel through the area to the CERT's staging location, then given to the CERT Team Leader; provides a summary of overall hazards in selected areas, including: • Fires; • Utility hazards; • Structural damage; • Injuries and deaths; • Available access; and • Essential for prioritizing and formulating action plans.
Personnel Resources Check-In [CERT Form #2]	Used to sign in CERT volunteers as they arrive at the staging location; provides information about: • Who is on site; • When they arrived; • When they were assigned; • Their special skills; and • Used by staging personnel to track personnel availability.
CERT Assignment Tracking Log [CERT Form #3]	Used by the Command Post for keeping awareness of situation status; contains essential information for tracking the overall situation.

Form	Purpose
Briefing Assignment [CERT Form #4 a, b]	Used by the Command Post to provide instructions to functional teams; used by teams to log their actions and report new damage assessment information.
Treatment Area Record [CERT Form #5]	Completed by medical treatment area personnel to record survivors entering the treatment area, their condition, and their status.
Communications Log [CERT Form #6 (based on ICS 309)]	Completed by the radio operator; used to log incoming and outgoing transmissions.
Equipment Inventory [CERT Form #7(based on ICS 303)]	Used to check out and check in CERT-managed equipment.
General Message [CERT Form #8 (ICS 213)]	Used for sending messages between command levels and groups; messages should be clear and concise and should focus on such key issues as: • Assignment completion; • Additional resources required; • Special information; and • Status update.

UNIT 2 SUMMARY

The key points from this unit are:

- Emergency response agencies and CERT use the ICS to manage emergency operations. ICS provides a flexible means of managing personnel, facilities, equipment, and communication and can be expanded when necessary.
- The key question CERT Team Leaders must always ask is: "Is it safe for CERT volunteers to attempt the rescue?" Whether or not to attempt a rescue depends on the degree of damage to the structure involved. Remember: CERT volunteers' safety is the top priority.
- It is vital to document and communicate information about situation and resource status to all CERT levels.
- Sections, Groups, and Teams must provide the Command Post with ongoing information about damage assessment, incident status, and ongoing needs.
- The Command Post must document the situation status, so the overall disaster situation can be tracked and reported to emergency response agencies.

Homework Assignment

Read and become familiar with the unit that will be covered in the next session.

CERT Unit 2: Additional Materials

Additional Materials:

- ☐ Damage Assessment
- ☐ Personnel Resources Check-In
- ☐ CERT Assignment Tracking Log
- ☐ Briefing Assignment
- ☐ Team Action Log
- ☐ Treatment Area Record
- ☐ Communications Log
- ☐ Equipment Inventory
- ☐ General Message

CERT UNIT 2: ADDITIONAL MATERIALS

CERT Damage Assessment Form

Form 2.9: CERT Damage Assessment Form

DAMAGE ASSESSMENT FORM	CERT		DATE	
LOCATION				

SIZE UP (check if applicable)															
FIRES		HAZARDS				STRUCTURE		PEOPLE			ROADS		ANIMALS		
BURNING	OUT	GAS LEAK	H20 LEAK	ELECTRIC	CHEMICAL	DAMAGED	COLLAPSED	INJURED	TRAPPED	DEAD	ACCESS	NC ACCESS	INJURED	TRAPPED	ROAMING

OBSERVATIONS

CERT Personnel Resources Check-In Form

Form 2.10: CERT Personnel Resources Check-In Form

PERSONNEL RESOURCES CHECK-IN			CERT								DATE		
CHECK IN TIME	CHECK OUT TIME	NAME	ID # (CERT badge or other)	CONTACT (cell # or radio)	PREFFERRED ASSIGNMENT				SKILLS			TEAM ASSIGNMENT	TIME ASSIGNED
					FIRE	MEDICAL	SAR						

CERT Assignment Tracking Log

Form 2.11: CERT Assignment Tracking Log

ASSIGNMENT TRACKING LOG	CERT		DATE
ASSIGNMENT	ASSIGNMENT	ASSIGNMENT	ASSIGNMENT
LOCATION	LOCATION	LOCATION	LOCATION
TEAM	TEAM	TEAM	TEAM
TEAM LEADER/CONTACT #	TEAM LEADER/CONTACT #	TEAM LEADER/CONTACT #	TEAM LEADER/CONTACT #
START TIME / END TIME	START TIME / END TIME	START TIME / END TIME	START TIME / END TIME
1	1	1	1
2	2	2	2
3	3	3	3
4	4	4	4
5	5	5	5
OBJECTIVES	OBJECTIVES	OBJECTIVES	OBJECTIVES
RESULTS	RESULTS	RESULTS	RESULTS

CERT LEADER

SCRIBE(S)

PAGE ___ OF ___

CERT Briefing Assignment Form

Form 2.12: CERT Briefing Assignment Form

BRIEFING ASSIGNMENT	CERT		DATE	
COMMAND POST CONTACT #			TIME OUT	TIME BACK
INSTRUCTIONS TO TEAM				
TEAM NAME	LOCATION			
OBJECTIVES				
EQUIPMENT ALLOCATED				

REPORT FROM RESPONSE TEAM

FIRES		HAZARDS				STRUCTURE		PEOPLE			ROADS		ANIMALS		
BURNING	OUT	GAS LEAK	H20 LEAK	ELECTRIC	CHEMICAL	DAMAGED	COLLAPSED	INJURED	TRAPPED	DEAD	ACCESS	NO ACCESS	INJURED	TRAPPED	ROAMING

CERT Team Action Log

Form 2.13: CERT Team Action Log

TEAM ACTION LOG
(time stamp each action; draw map if needed)

CERT Victim Treatment Area Record

Form 2.14: CERT Victim Treatment Area Record

VICTIM TREATMENT AREA RECORD	CERT	DATE
TREATMENT AREA LOCATION		

TIME IN	NAME OR DESCRIPTION	CONDITION/TREATMENT (update as needed)	MOVED TO	TIME OUT
SCRIBE(S)			PAGE ___ OF ____	

CERT Communications Log

Form 2.15: CERT Communications Log

| Communications Log | CERT | DATE |
| | | |

| RADIO OPERATOR NAME | | |

LOG

TIME	FROM	TO	MESSAGE

CERT Equipment Inventory Form

Form 2.16: CERT Equipment Inventory Log

EQUIPMENT INVENTORY		CERT				DATE			
ASSET #	ITEM DESCRIPTION	OWNER	ISSUED TO		QTY	TIME	INITIALS	COMMENTS	
				ISSUED					
				RETURNED					
				ISSUED					
				RETURNED					
				ISSUED					
				RETURNED					
				ISSUED					
				RETURNED					
				ISSUED					
				RETURNED					
				ISSUED					
				RETURNED					
				ISSUED					
				RETURNED					
				ISSUED					
				RETURNED					
				ISSUED					
				RETURNED					
				ISSUED					
				RETURNED					
				ISSUED					
				RETURNED					
				ISSUED					
				RETURNED					
SCRIBE(S)						PAGE ___ OF ___			

CERT General Message Form

Form 2.17: CERT General Message Form

GENERAL MESSAGE	
TO	POSITION
FROM	POSITION
SUBJECT	DATE / TIME

MESSAGE

SIGNATURE	POSITION

REPLY

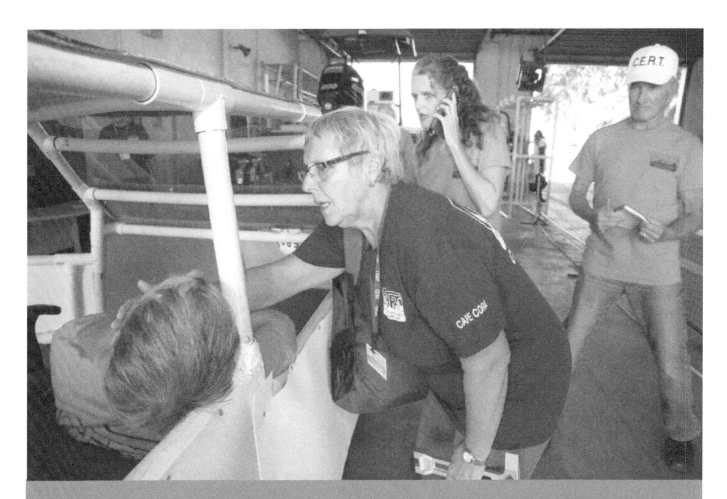

CERT Unit 3: Disaster Medical Operations – Part 1

Participant Manual

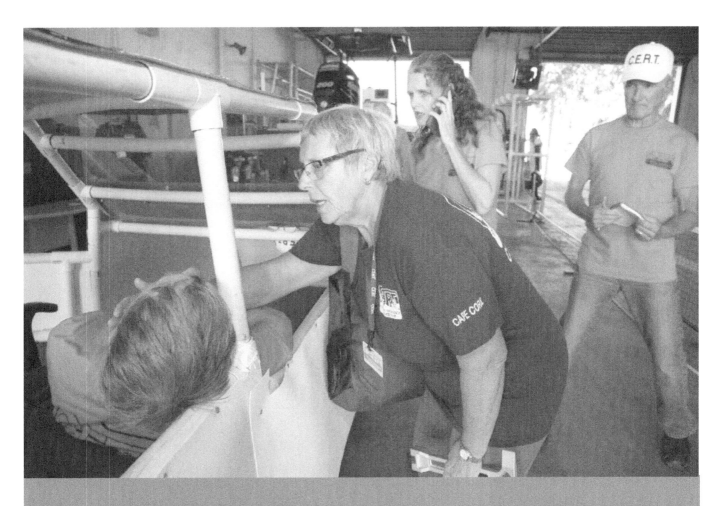

CERT Unit 3: Disaster Medical Operations – Part 1

In this unit, you will learn about:

☐ **Assisting Disaster Medical Operations**: How to assist by controlling bleeding, maintaining normal body temperature, opening an airway, providing comfort to patients, and applying basic first aid care for a number of injuries.

CERT Unit 3 Table of Contents

SECTION 1: UNIT 3 OVERVIEW

Understanding the medical operations environment in a disaster is crucial to CERT's success in assisting emergency responders. Units 3 and 4, Disaster Medical Operations Part I and II, teach life-saving steps CERT volunteers can take immediately following trauma. It also provides an overview of how emergency responders apply and organize disaster medical care in the event of a large-scale disaster. CERT volunteer's assistance with disaster medical operations can play a vital role in limiting deaths from trauma.

Units 3 and 4 do not provide an absolute way of how to manage disaster medical operations. Many localities will handle disaster medical operations differently, and there is not one concrete way to teach this material. Instead, the goal of Units 3 and 4 is to provide a high-level overview about the immediate medical interventions CERT volunteers can take to save lives, including how disaster medical operations may operate.

In a disaster, there may be more survivors than rescuers, and assistance from medical professionals may not be immediately available. While emergency medical responders are quick to arrive, any delay between injury and the initiation of care can result in death. Those nearest to someone with life-threatening injuries are in the best position to provide the first care, which should focus on the most essential actions. These essential actions include moving someone away from ongoing danger, stopping life-threatening bleeding, positioning the injured so they can breathe, keeping them warm, and providing comfort.

CERT volunteers are trained to be part of disaster medical operations and to assist in providing treatment for life-threatening conditions. Remember, the mission of CERT is to provide the greatest good for the greatest number of people. In a disaster with many survivors, time will be critical. CERT volunteers must work quickly and efficiently to help as many survivors as possible.

All CERT participants are encouraged to take basic first aid and CPR training; however, even if you have taken first aid courses you will need to understand CERT covers basic medical interventions for life-threatening (traumatic) injuries. This course does not teach CPR. To find a CPR course near you, search your local chapters of the American Red Cross and American Heart Association.

Unit Objectives

At the end of this unit, you should be able to:

1. Identify life-threatening conditions resulting from trauma including severe bleeding, low body temperature, and airway blockage;
2. Apply correct life saving techniques; and
3. Provide basic first-aid care for non-life-threatening injuries.

SECTION 2: TREATING LIFE-THREATENING CONDITIONS

Without treatment, severe bleeding and airway obstruction can quickly lead to death. The first priority of CERT volunteers assisting in disaster medical operations is to attend to these conditions by controlling bleeding and properly position a patient, so they can breathe.

Prior to treatment, it is critical to ensure that both the survivor and rescuer are in a safe environment to administer care. CERT volunteers should use their best judgement to determine if the situation is safe enough to help a survivor.

Some questions CERT volunteers can consider are:

- Do I feel safe at this spot?
- Should I leave a move to a safer location, or am I able to stay and start providing care immediately?
- If I leave, can I take anyone with me?

Whatever the decision is, the goal is to get help to the people who need it as soon as possible.

Approaching the Patient

When able, CERT volunteers should first ensure they are wearing the appropriate and proper personal protective equipment (PPE). For a detailed list of PPE, please reference Unit 1.

There are several steps to take when approaching a patient.

Step 1: If the patient is conscious, be sure he or she can see you.

Step 2: Identify yourself by giving your name and indicating the organization with which you are affiliated.

Step 3: Always request permission to treat an individual. If the individual is unconscious, it is assumed that the patient has given "implied consent," and you may treat him or her. Ask a parent or guardian for permission to treat a child, if possible.

Step 4: Whenever possible, respect cultural differences.

Step 5: Remember, all medical patients are legally entitled to confidentiality (HIPAA). When dealing with patients, always be mindful and respectful of the privacy of their medical condition.

Controlling Bleeding

The average person has approximately five liters of blood. Severe blood loss can result in irreversible shock. This means that if you lose about half of your body's blood supply, no matter what anyone does to try to save you, death is unavoidable. You must get bleeding under control as soon as possible.

Indications of life-threatening bleeding include:

- Spurting/steady bleeding;
- Blood is pooling;
- Blood is soaking through overlying clothes;
- Blood is soaking through bandages; and
- Amputation.

Life-threatening decreases in blood pressure often are associated with a state of shock. There are typically four stages of excessive bleeding.

Stage 1: Loss of <15% of blood volume. Patient appears normal with a slightly increased heart rate.

Stage 2: Loss of 15%-30% of blood volume. Patient's body is able to compensate for the loss of blood but may appear agitated or anxious as vital signs rise.

Stage 3: Loss of 30%-40% of blood volume. Patient becomes unable to compensate and condition worsens. If left untreated will proceed to irreversible shock. Patient appears confused.

Stage 4: Loss of >40% of blood volume. Patient enters irreversible shock. Patient appears lethargic and death will occur within minutes because of overwhelming and irreversible damage to vital organs.

Table 3.1: Stages of Severe Bleeding

Stage	Blood Loss	Heart Rate	Blood Pressure	Breath Rate	Patient
I	Less than 15%	Normal (<100 bpm)	Normal	14-20	Patient appears normal
II	15%-40%	Fast (>100 bpm)	Slightly Low	20-30	Patient may feel anxious
III	30%-40%	Very Fast (>120 bpm)	Low	30-40	Patient feels confused
IV	Greater than 40%	Critical (>140 bpm)	Critical	>35	Patient feels lethargic

Types of bleeding are characterized by the speed of the blood flow.

Arterial bleeding: Arteries transport blood under high pressure. Blood coming from an artery will spurt.

Venous bleeding: Veins transport blood under low pressure. Blood coming from a vein will flow.

Capillary bleeding: Capillaries also carry blood under low pressure. Blood coming from capillaries will ooze.

Direct Pressure

The first way to try to control excessive bleeding is through applying direct pressure. To control and stop bleeding through direct pressure, follow the steps below.

Step 1: Find the source(s) of bleeding.

Step 2: If you have something to put in between the blood and your hands, use it. (e.g., gloves, a cloth, a plastic bag.)

Step 3: Apply firm, steady pressure directly on the source of the bleeding. Push hard to stop or slow bleeding—even if it is painful to the injured!

Step 4: Keep pressure applied until EMS takes over care or bleeding has stopped. If you are unsure if bleeding has stopped, continue applying pressure and wait for EMS.

Some things to keep in mind when applying direct pressure:

- Try to provide a barrier against the blood, if possible. Gloves are best.
- Do **not** use the same gloves or barrier on more than one person.
- If your barrier becomes blood soaked, replace it, but do not layer more things on top of it.
- Do **not** place bulky layers in between your hands and the source of the wound because it decreases the effectiveness of the pressure.
- Correctly applied pressure may not be comfortable for the injured. Do not let up; hold pressure until EMS arrives.

Tourniquets

If you cannot stop the bleeding by applying direct pressure and EMS professionals are delayed in responding, a tourniquet may be a viable option to save a person from bleeding to death. Tourniquets have been used effectively in combat to control bleeding in a wounded soldier's extremities (arms or legs) and are increasingly being used by uniformed responders in civilian emergencies. Tourniquets are safe and effective when applied appropriately; you are more likely to save a life than cause the loss of a limb if you use a tourniquet.

A tourniquet is a tight bandage, which when placed around a limb and tightened, cuts off the blood supply to the part of the limb beyond it.

If a commercial tourniquet is not readily available, you can try to create one yourself using something that is broad, flexible, strong, and able to be twisted, tightened, and secured, such as a webbed belt or luggage strap or material. Improvised tourniquets often fail, but you can attempt to use them as a last resort to at least slow the bleeding.

How to use a tourniquet:

Step 1: Place as high as possible on the injured limb – closest to the torso. (You can place it over clothing.)

Step 2: Pull the strap through the buckle.

Step 3: Twist the rod tightly until bleeding stops/slows significantly. (May be very painful.)

Step 4: Secure the rod.

Step 5: If bleeding does not stop, place a second tourniquet.

Step 6: Leave in place until EMS takes over care.

Image 3.1: Tourniquet

Recognizing Shock

The body will initially compensate for blood loss and mask the symptoms of shock; therefore, shock is often difficult to diagnose. It is possible — and, in fact, common — for an individual suffering from shock to be fully coherent and not complaining of pain. Pay attention to subtle clues, as failure to recognize shock will have serious consequences.

Main signs of shock:

- Rapid and shallow breathing;
- Capillary refill of greater than two seconds; and
- Failure to follow simple commands, such as "squeeze my hand."

When a patient is in shock, avoid rough or excessive handling. It is also important to maintain the patient's body temperature.

Maintaining Body Temperature

If necessary, place a blanket or other material under and/or over the patient to provide protection from extreme ground temperatures (hot or cold). People with very serious injuries are more susceptible to hypothermia, or abnormally low body temperature. Hypothermia increases the risk of death in survivors with serious injuries, so you must maintain normal body temperatures in patients as much as possible.

To keep a person warm, you should:

- Remove wet clothing;

- Place something between the injured person and the ground (e.g., cardboard, jacket, blanket, or anything that provides physical separation);
- Wrap the injured person with dry layers (e.g., coat, blanket, or Mylar emergency blanket); and
- Shield the injured person from the wind with your body or surrounding objects.

Hypothermia and other cold-related injuries will be discussed in greater detail later in this unit.

Exercise 3.1: Controlling Bleeding

Purpose: This exercise will provide a chance to practice using the techniques for controlling bleeding.

Instructions:

1. After breaking into pairs, identify one person to take the role of the patient and one to take the role of the rescuer.
2. Respond as if the patient has an injury on the right forearm, just below the elbow.
3. Apply a pressure bandage or tourniquet (if available).
4. Repeat the process twice.
5. Swap roles and have the new rescuer complete the above steps.

Opening the Airway

Positioning an injured patient to keep their airway open and clear is critical to saving their life. The best position for the body is one in which the chest can expand fully, and the airway is not at risk of being obstructed. In other words, the best position is one in which the tongue cannot flop back into the individual's throat and one in which blood or fluid does not end up in the lungs (aspirated), particularly in the case with someone with facial trauma.

The respiratory system includes the following components:

- Lung;
- Bronchus;
- Larynx;
- Pharynx;
- Nasal Cavity; and
- Trachea.

There are different ways to position an injured patient to keep their airway open depending on if the patient is conscious or unconscious.

Positioning a Conscious Patient

Someone who is awake will naturally assume the position that is best for them given their injuries. Despite how it looks to you, let them self-manage their airway by positioning their own body. Assist if needed.

The tripod position is a natural way to open your airway – think of catching your breath after sprinting. In the tripod position, the lungs and ribcage are able to expand as fully as possible.

- **When sitting on a raised platform** (e.g., chair, bench): Legs shoulder width apart, elbows or hands on knees, and leaning forward slightly.
- **When standing:** Legs shoulder width apart, hands on knees arms straight, and leaning forward with flat back.

Positioning an Unconscious Patient

If an individual is unconscious, you can help by turning the person on his or her side so their chest can expand, tilting the head to drain fluid away from the airway. To assess an unconscious patient, consider the following diagram:

Image 3.2: Positioning an Unconscious Patient

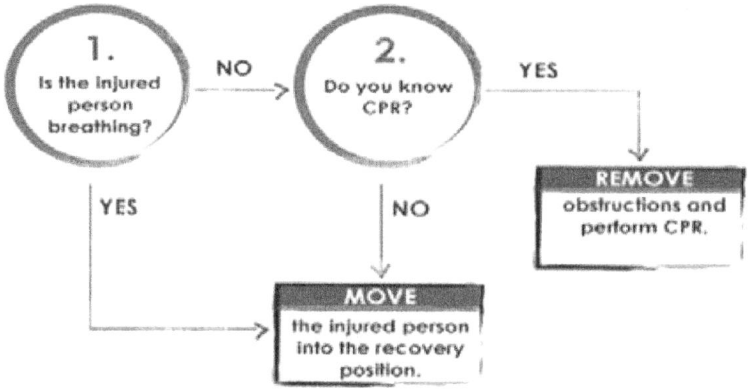

Recovery Position

If you decide to move a patient into the recovery position, place the patient's body like this:

- Body: Laid on its side;
- Bottom Arm: Reached outward;
- Top Arm: Rest hand on bicep of bottom arm;
- Head: Rest on hand;
- Legs: Bent slightly;
- Chin: Raised forward; and
- Mouth: Pointed downward.

Although the risk is very small, it is possible that moving someone into the recovery position could cause harm to the person's spine. To prevent this:

- Try to support the head and neck when rolling them onto their side.
- Do **not** move them more than necessary.

Jaw-thrust Maneuver

When the patient is unconscious, and you suspect there is an airway obstruction, clear the airway using the jaw-thrust maneuver.

To perform this maneuver on an adult, kneel above the patient's head and:

- Put one hand on each side of the patient's head with the thumbs near the corners of the mouth pointed toward the chin, using the elbows for support.
- Slide the fingers into position under the angles of the patient's jawbone without moving the head or neck.
- Thrust the jaw upward without moving the head or neck to lift the jaw and open the airway.

Exercise 3.2: Recovery Position

Purpose: This exercise will provide a chance to practice using the techniques for moving a patient into the recovery position.

Instructions:

1. Break into pairs and have one person play the rescuer and one person play the patient.
2. Assume the unconscious injured individual is breathing.
3. Place them into the recovery position using the technique you just learned.

Providing Comfort

CERT volunteers can be of great value to injured and emotional patients simply by offering comfort and support. No special skills are needed—just a calm and reassuring presence. Unit 5 will discuss disaster psychology in greater depth; however, it is important to note that providing comfort is a part of the immediate care CERT volunteers can provide.

A Dialogue for Providing Comfort

Share names and ask basic questions, for example:

- How can I help?
- What do you need?
- What happened?

You can also provide comfort to the patient by supplying information about:

- What you currently know about what happened without speculating;
- What is being done to assist them; and
- What is going to happen next.

What can you do?

- Keep them warm.
- Offer a hand to hold.
- Maintain eye contact.
- Be patient and understanding.
- If you have to move on to provide aid to another person, let him or her know.

SECTION 3: BASIC FIRST-AID CARE

Treating Burns

The first step in treating burns is to conduct a thorough size-up. A few examples of burn-related size-up questions to ask are:

- What caused the burn?
- Is the danger still present?
- When did the burning cease?

The objectives of first aid treatment for burns are to:

- Prevent hypothermia;
- Manage pain; and
- Reduce the risk of infection.

Heat, chemicals, electrical current, or radiation may cause burns. The severity of a burn depends on the:

- Temperature of the burning agent;
- Period of time the patient was exposed;
- Area of the body that was affected;
- Size of the area burned; and
- Depth of the burn.

Burn Classifications

Depending on the severity, burns may affect all three layers of skin.

1. The epidermis, or outer layer of skin, contains nerve endings and is penetrated by hairs.
2. The dermis, or middle layer of skin, contains blood vessels, oil glands, hair follicles, and sweat glands.
3. The subcutaneous layer, or innermost layer, contains blood vessels and overlies the muscles.

Table 3.2: Burn Classification Chart

Classification	Skin Layers Affected	Signs
Superficial	• Epidermis	• Reddened, dry skin • Pain • Swelling (possible)
Partial Thickness	• Epidermis • Partial destruction of dermis	• Reddened, blistered skin • Wet appearance • Pain • Swelling (possible)
Full Thickness	• Complete destruction of epidermis and dermis	• Whitened, leathery, or charred (brown or black)

Classification	Skin Layers Affected	Signs
	• Possible subcutaneous damage (destroys all layers of skin and some or all underlying structures)	• Painful or relatively painless

Guidelines for Treating Heat Burns

Cool the burn:

- Remove the patient from the burning source. Put out any flames and remove smoldering clothing unless it is stuck to the skin.
- Cool skin or clothing, if they are still hot, by immersing them in cool water for not more than one minute or covering with clean compresses that have been soaked in cool water and wrung out. ***Note** that rapid temperature changes can cause shock in the patient, so it is important to assess the size and severity of the burn prior to attempting to cool the skin to prevent a drop-in body temperature.*
- Cooling sources include water from the bathroom or kitchen; garden hose; and soaked towels, sheets, or other cloths.
- Do **not** use ice. Ice causes vessel constriction.

Dress the burn:

- Cover loosely with dry, sterile dressings to keep air out, reduce pain, and prevent infection.
- Wrap fingers and toes loosely and individually when treating severe burns to the hands and feet.
- Loosen clothing near the affected area. Remove jewelry if necessary, taking care to document what you removed, when, and to whom you gave it.
- Do **not** apply antiseptics, ointments, or other remedies.
- Do **not** remove shreds of tissue, break blisters, or remove adhered particles of clothing (cut burned-in clothing around the burn.)

Guidelines for Treating Chemical Burns

Unlike more traditional burns, chemical burns do not result from extreme heat, and therefore, treatment differs greatly (e.g., decontamination procedures). If you suspect a chemical burn, it is best to defer treatment to trained medical professionals.

Chemical burns are not always obvious. Consider chemical burns as a possibility if the patient's skin is burning and there is no sign of a fire. If you suspect a chemical burn:

- Protect yourself from contact with the substance. Use your protective gear, especially goggles, mask, and gloves;
- Be sure to remove any affected clothing or jewelry;
- If the irritant is dry, gently brush away as much as possible. Always brush away from the eyes and away from the patient and yourself;
- Use lots of cool running water to flush the chemical from the skin for at least 10 minutes. The running water will dilute the chemical fast enough to prevent the injury from getting worse;

- Apply a cool, wet compress to relieve pain; and
- Cover the wound very loosely with a dry, sterile, or clean cloth so that the cloth will not stick to the wound.

Wound Care

The main treatment for wounds includes:

- Control bleeding; and
- Apply dressing and bandage.

Treatment for controlling bleeding was covered earlier in this unit. The focus of this section is on bandaging, which will help to prevent secondary infection.

Bandaging Wounds

Once you have controlled bleeding, you will need to apply a dressing and bandage to help maintain the clot and prevent infection.

There is a difference between a dressing and a bandage:

- Apply dressing directly to the wound. Whenever possible, a dressing should be sterile; and
- A bandage holds the dressing in place.

If a wound is still bleeding, the bandage should place enough pressure on the wound to help control bleeding without interfering with circulation.

Rules of Dressing

The rules of dressing are:

- If there is active bleeding (i.e., if the dressing is soaked with blood), redress over the existing dressing and maintain pressure to control bleeding; and
- In the absence of active bleeding, maintain the pressure and keep the wound bandaged until further treatment by a medical professional.

Signs of possible infection include:

- Swelling around the wound site;
- Discoloration;
- Discharge from the wound; and
- Red striations from the wound site.

Amputations

If CERT volunteers are assisting a patient with a severed body part there are a few guidelines to follow. Note that CERT volunteers should never amputate a body part. When the severed body part can be located, CERT volunteers should:

- Save tissue parts, wrapped in clean material and placed in a plastic bag, if available. Label them with the date, time, and patient's name;
- Keep the tissue parts cool, but NOT in direct contact with ice; and
- Keep the severed body part with the patient.

Impaled Objects

Sometimes, you may also encounter some patients who have foreign objects lodged in their bodies, usually as the result of flying debris. This situation is usually outside the scope of CERT training. The best course of action is to find trained medical personnel (EMS) to care for a patient with an impaled object. However, in the event that EMS is still a long way from the scene or otherwise unavailable, there are a few steps you can take to provide care.

When a foreign object impales a patient, you should:

- Immobilize the affected body part;
- Not attempt to move or remove the object, unless it is obstructing the airway;
- Try to control bleeding at the entrance wound without placing undue pressure on the foreign object;
- Clean and dress the wound making sure to stabilize the impaled object; and
- Wrap bulky dressings around the object to keep it from moving.

Treating Fractures, Dislocations, Sprains, and Strains

The objective when treating a suspected fracture, sprain, or strain is to immobilize the injury and the joints immediately above and below the injury site. Because it is difficult to distinguish among fractures, sprains, or strains, if uncertain of the type of injury, CERT members should treat the injury as a fracture.

Fractures

A fracture is a complete break, a chip, or a crack in a bone. There are several types of fractures.

- An **open fracture** is a broken bone with some kind of wound that allows contaminants to enter into or around the fracture site.
- A **closed fracture** is a broken bone with no associated wound. First aid treatment for closed fractures may require only splinting.

Image 3.3: Open and Closed Fractures

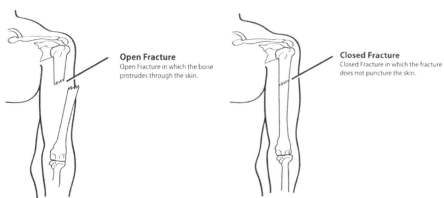

Open Fracture
Open Fracture in which the bone protrudes through the skin.

Closed Fracture
Closed Fracture in which the fracture does not puncture the skin.

If the limb is angled, then it is a **displaced fracture**, which can be described by the degree of displacement of the bone fragments.

Nondisplaced fractures are difficult to identify, with the main signs being pain and swelling. You should treat a suspected fracture as a fracture until professional treatment is available.

Image 3.4: Displaced and Nondisplaced Fractures

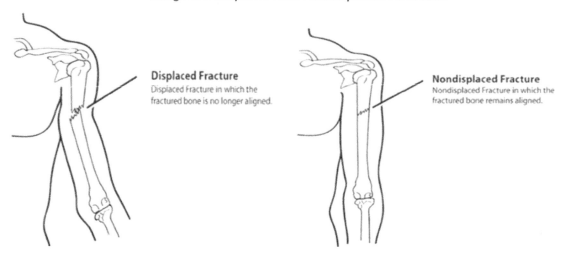

Displaced Fracture
Displaced Fracture in which the fractured bone is no longer aligned.

Nondisplaced Fracture
Nondisplaced Fracture in which the fractured bone remains aligned.

Treating an Open Fracture

Closed fractures are generally treated with splinting, but open fractures are more dangerous because they pose a significant risk of severe bleeding and infection. Therefore, they are a higher priority and volunteers should check them more frequently.

When treating an open fracture:

- Do **not** draw the exposed bone ends back into the tissue; and
- Do **not** irrigate the wound.

You should:

- Cover the wound with a sterile dressing and apply pressure;
- Splint the fracture without disturbing the wound; and
- Place a moist 4 by 4-inch dressing over the bone end to keep it from drying out.

Dislocations

Dislocations are another common injury in emergencies. A dislocation is an injury to the ligaments around a joint that is so severe that it permits a separation of the bone from its normal position in a joint.

The signs of a dislocation are similar to those of a closed fracture, and you should treat a suspected dislocation like a closed fracture.

You should not try to relocate a suspected dislocation. You should immobilize the joint until professional medical help is available.

Sprains and Strains

A sprain involves a stretching or tearing of ligaments at a joint. Typically, stretching or extending the joint beyond its normal limits causes the sprain.

A sprain is considered a partial dislocation, although the bone either remains in place or is able to fall back into place after the injury. Whether an injury is a strain, sprain, or closed fracture, treat the injury as if it is a closed fracture.

The most common signs of a sprain are:

- Tenderness at the site of the injury;
- Swelling and/or bruising; and
- Restricted use or loss of use.

Splinting

Splinting is the most common procedure for immobilizing an injury.

Cardboard is the most common type of material used for makeshift splints, but a variety of materials can be used, including:

- **Soft materials:** Towels, blankets, or pillows, tied with bandaging materials or soft cloths; and
- **Rigid materials:** A board, metal strip, folded magazine or newspaper, or another rigid item.

Volunteers can create anatomical splints by securing a fractured bone to an adjacent un-fractured bone. Usually, anatomical splints are reserved for fingers and toes, but, in an emergency, volunteers may splint legs together.

Use soft materials to fill the gap between the splinting material and the body part.

With this type of injury, there will be swelling. Remove restrictive clothing, shoes, and jewelry when necessary to prevent these items from acting as unintended tourniquets.

Splint Illustrations

Image 3.5: Cardboard Splint

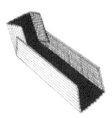

To create a cardboard splint, turn up the edges of the cardboard to form a "mold" in which the injured limb can rest.

Image 3.5: Cardboard Splint

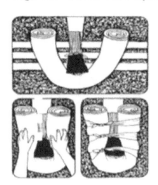

To splint using a towel, roll up the towel and wrap it around the limb, then tie it in place.

Image 3.7: Pillow Splint

For a pillow splint, wrap and tie the pillow around the limb.

Image 3.8: Anatomical Splint

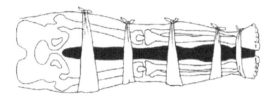

An anatomical splint is one in which the injured leg is tied at intervals to the non-injured leg, using a blanket as padding between the legs.

Exercise 3.3: Splinting

Purpose: This exercise will provide you with a chance to practice splinting techniques.

Instructions:

1. Break down into groups of two. One person will play the rescuer, the other person will be the patient.
2. The rescuer will place a splint on the patient's upper arm, and then one on the patient's lower leg.
3. After several observed attempts at splinting, the rescuer and the patient will swap roles.

Treating Cold-Related Injuries

Cold-related injuries include:

- **Hypothermia**, which is a condition that occurs when the body's temperature drops below normal; and
- **Frostbite**, which occurs when extreme cold shuts down blood flow to extremities, causing tissue death.

Hypothermia

Hypothermia may be caused by exposure to cold or by trauma. The primary signs and symptoms of hypothermia are:

- A body temperature of 95° F (37° C) or lower;
- Redness or blueness of the skin; and
- Numbness accompanied by shivering.

In later stages, hypothermia will be accompanied by:

- Slurred speech;
- Unpredictable behavior; and
- Listlessness.

Because hypothermia can set in within only a few minutes, treat patients rescued from cold air or water environments first by:

- Removing wet clothing;
- Placing something between the injured person and the ground (e.g., cardboard, jacket, blanket, or anything that provides physical separation);
- Wrapping the injured person with dry layers (e.g., coat, blanket, or Mylar emergency blanket);
- Shielding the injured person from the wind with your body or surrounding objects;
- Not attempting to use massage to warm affected body parts; and
- Placing an unconscious patient in the recovery position.

Frostbite

A person's blood vessels constrict in cold weather in an effort to preserve body heat. In extreme cold, the body will further constrict blood vessels in the extremities in an effort to shunt blood toward the core organs (e.g., heart, lungs, intestines). The combination of inadequate circulation and extreme temperatures will cause tissue in these extremities to freeze, and in some cases, tissue death will result. Frostbite is most common in the nose, ears, hands, and feet.

There are several key signs and symptoms of frostbite:

- Skin discoloration (red, white, purple, black);
- Burning or tingling sensation, at times not localized to the injury site; and
- Partial or complete numbness.

Warm a patient suffering from frostbite slowly! Thawing the frozen extremity too rapidly can cause chilled blood to flow to the heart, shocking it, and potentially stopping it.

- Immerse injured area in warm (NOT hot) water, approximately 107.6° F.
- **DO NOT** allow the body part to re-freeze, as this will exacerbate the injury.
- **DO NOT** attempt to use massage to warm body parts. Frostbite results in the formation of ice crystals in the tissue; rubbing could potentially cause a great deal of damage!

Wrap affected body parts in dry, sterile dressing. Again, it is vital to complete this task carefully to reduce the likelihood of further tissue damage.

Treating Heat-Related Injuries

As a CERT volunteer, you may encounter several types of heat-related injuries during a disaster, including the following:

- **Heat cramps:** muscle spasms brought on by over-exertion in extreme heat.
- **Heat exhaustion:** occurs when an individual exercises or works in extreme heat, resulting in loss of body fluids through heavy sweating. Blood flow to the skin increases, causing blood flow to decrease to the vital organs. This results in a mild form of shock.
- **Heat stroke**: life-threatening condition when the patient's temperature control system shuts down, and body temperature can rise so high that brain damage and death may result.

Heat Exhaustion

The symptoms of heat exhaustion are:

- Cool, moist, pale, or flushed skin;
- Heavy sweating;
- Headache;
- Nausea or vomiting;
- Dizziness; and/or
- Exhaustion.

A patient suffering heat exhaustion will have a near normal body temperature. If left untreated, heat exhaustion will develop into heat stroke.

Heat Stroke

Some or all of the following symptoms characterize heat stroke:

- Hot, red skin;
- Lack of perspiration;
- Changes in consciousness; and/or
- Rapid, weak pulse and rapid, shallow breathing.

In a heat stroke patient, body temperature can be very high — as high as 105° F. If an individual suffering from heat stroke is not treated, death can result.

Treatment

Treatment is similar for both heat exhaustion and heat stroke.

1. Take the patient out of the heat and place in a cool environment.
2. Cool the body slowly with cool, wet towels or sheets. If possible, put the patient in a cool bath.
3. Have a heat stroke patient drink water, SLOWLY, at the rate of approximately half a glass of water every 15 minutes. Consuming too much water too quickly will cause nausea and vomiting in a patient of heat sickness.
4. If the patient is experiencing vomiting, cramping, or is losing consciousness, **DO NOT** administer food or drink. Alert a medical professional as soon as possible and keep a close watch on the individual until professional help is available.

Insect Bites and Stings

In a disaster environment, insect bites and stings may be more common than is typical as these creatures, like people, are under additional stress.

The specific symptoms vary depending on the type of creature, but generally, bites and stings can result in redness and itching, tingling or burning at the site of the injury, and often a welt on the skin at the site.

Treatment for insect bites and stings follows the steps below.

Step 1: Remove the stinger if still present by scraping the edge of a credit card or other stiff, straight-edged object across the stinger. Do not use tweezers; these may squeeze the venom sac and increase the amount of venom released.

Step 2: Wash the site thoroughly with soap and water.

Step 3: Place ice (wrapped in a washcloth) on the site of the sting for 10 minutes and then off for 10 minutes. Repeat this process.

Allergic Reactions to Bites and Stings

The greatest concern with any insect bite or sting is a severe allergic reaction, or anaphylaxis. Anaphylaxis occurs when an allergic reaction becomes so severe that it compromises the airway. If you suspect anaphylaxis:

- Calm the individual;
- If possible, find and help administer a patient's Epi-pen. (Many severe allergy sufferers carry one at all times); and
- **DO NOT** administer medicine aside from the Epi-pen. This includes pain relievers, allergy medicine, etc.

UNIT 3 SUMMARY

The key points from this unit are:

- CERT volunteers' ability to provide first, live-saving measures can be critical during a disaster.
- Life-saving measures CERT volunteers can take, include:
  - Controlling severe bleeding using direct pressure and/or a tourniquet;
  - Maintaining normal body temperature; and
  - Opening airways and positioning patients correctly.
- CERT volunteers can be of great value to injured and emotional patients simply by offering comfort and support. No special skills are needed — just a calm and reassuring presence.
- In addition to critical life-saving measures, CERT volunteers can also administer basic first aid and care to injured patients.
- Other injuries that are common after disasters:
  - Burns;
  - Wounds;
  - Amputations and impaled objects;
  - Fractures, dislocations, sprains, and strains;
  - Cold-related injuries;
  - Heat-related injuries; and
  - Insect bites/stings.

Homework Assignment

Read and become familiar with Unit 4: Disaster Medical Operations — Part 2 before the next session.

CERT Unit 4: Disaster Medical Operations – Part 2

Participant Manual

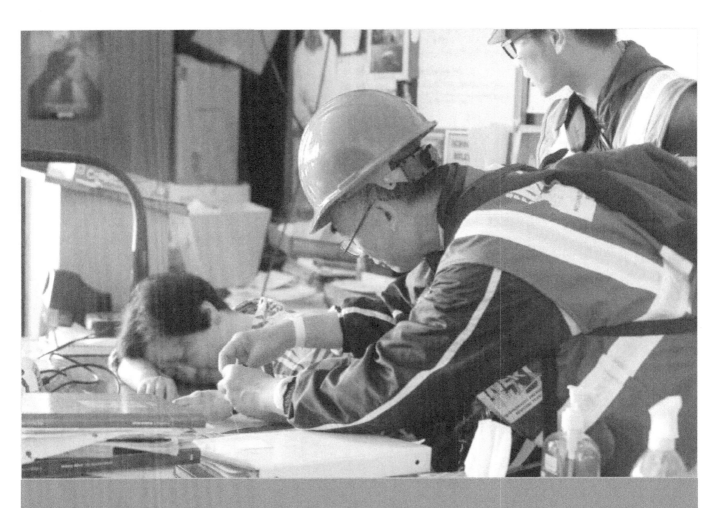

CERT Unit 4: Disaster Medical Operations – Part 2

In this unit you will learn about:

- **Mass Casualty Incidents:** How to assist first responders in responding to mass casualty incidents.

- **Functions of Disaster Medical Operations:** Major functions of disaster medical operations.

- **Disaster Medical Treatment Areas:** Types of medical treatment areas.

- **Head-to-Toe Assessment:** How to perform a head-to-toe assessment to identify and treat injuries.

- **Public Health Considerations:** How to maintain hygiene and sanitation.

CERT Unit 4 Table of Contents

SECTION 1: UNIT 4 OVERVIEW

Unit Objectives

At the end of this unit, you should be able to:

1. Explain the role of the CERT volunteer during a mass casualty incident;
2. Describe the functions of disaster medical operations;
3. Describe how to set up survivor treatment areas;
4. Perform head-to-toe patient assessments; and
5. Take appropriate sanitation and hygiene measures to protect public health.

SECTION 2: MASS CASUALTY INCIDENTS

Mass casualty incidents are incidents in which the number of casualties overwhelms local resources. While these incidents are infrequent, CERT volunteers can play an important role by supporting local resources in responding to the incident.

Examples of mass casualty incidents include:

- Commuter train derailment;
- Multi-car accident;
- Bus accident;
- Building collapse; and
- Natural disasters (e.g., tornadoes).

In mass casualty incidents, first responder personnel:

- Establish command and control of the incident area;
- Conduct a scene size-up and set-up;
- Send survivors with relatively minor injuries to a holding area to await treatment;
- Identify survivors who require life-saving interventions and treat them immediately;
- Identify deceased victims as well as survivors too severely injured to save;
- Manage medical transportation for survivors who require additional treatment;
- Secure the area to protect first responders, survivors, and evidence for law enforcement investigations; and
- Remove debris and other safety or health threats.

In addition to providing critical life-saving interventions, first responders must organize a likely chaotic situation when they arrive on scene. To support first responders, CERT volunteers must understand their role during mass casualty incidents.

Role of CERT Volunteers during Mass Casualty Incidents

Whether dispatched to the scene or located nearby by coincidence, the first task of a CERT volunteer is to conduct a scene size-up. Take a moment to look around the scene and determine the appropriate course of action.

- Call 9-1-1 and provide the operator with the information gathered during your initial size-up.
- Put on your personal protective equipment (PPE), and any CERT affiliated gear, such as a hat, vest, or shirt.
- Locate the nearest first responder and identify yourself as a CERT volunteer. Give them your local agency affiliation.
- If a first responder is not available, assess the situation and determine whether you can provide life-saving interventions, such as controlling bleeding or opening an airway.
- Once responders have arrived, provide them with detailed information from your size-up, and ask how you may be of assistance. Again, communicate your CERT affiliation to first responder personnel.

- For your safety, first responders may ask you to leave the area. After leaving, report the incident and your role to your CERT Team Leader and/or local agency CERT affiliation.
- Communication is key for supporting first responders. CERT volunteers can provide valuable information to support an effective response.

SECTION 3: FUNCTIONS OF DISASTER MEDICAL OPERATIONS

Disaster medical operations are the tasks associated with survivor treatment and support during a mass casualty incident. The major functions of disaster medical operations are:

- **Triage/Assessment:** The initial assessment and sorting of survivors for treatment based on the severity of their injuries;
- **Treatment:** The medical services provided to survivors;
- **Transport:** The movement of survivors from the scene to the treatment area or medical facility;
- **Morgue:** The temporary holding area for patients who died at the scene or the treatment area; and
- **Supply:** The hub for getting and distributing supplies.

Image 4.11: Disaster Medical Operations Organization

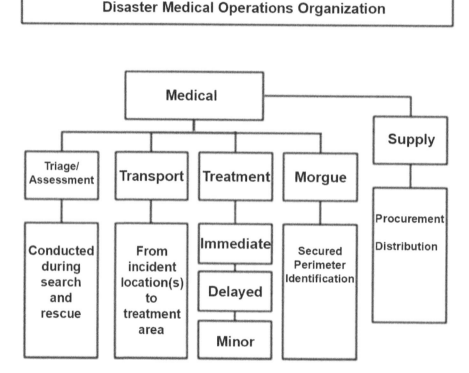

Disaster Medical Operations Organization showing the functions of disaster medical operations: Triage/Assessment, Transport, Treatment, Morgue, and Supply

Triage/assessment and transport are functions of both search and rescue operations and medical operations.

SECTION 4: ESTABLISHING MEDICAL TREATMENT AREAS

As soon as injured survivors are confirmed, first responders will begin to set up one or more treatment area(s). The location of treatment areas will take into consideration safety for rescuers and survivors, as well as, ease of access to resources (e.g., medical supplies, transport areas). First responders may call on CERT volunteers to help establish treatment areas or supply needs.

Decentralized Treatment Areas: It is sometimes necessary to set up more than one medical treatment location. The severity of the damage, number of injuries and casualties, and the safety of the immediate environment determine where the initial treatment area(s) should be located. Having multiple treatment areas can provide life-saving interventions when a central location is too far away from the initial treatment area.

- A medical treatment location should be set up a safe distance from, but not too far from, each of the damage sites.
- Each treatment location should include physically separated treatment areas for survivors and a morgue.
- Survivors remain under treatment at the location until first responders can transport them to a location for professional medical care.

Centralized Treatment Areas: In an event with few injured survivors at several sites, first responders may need to establish one central medical treatment location. A centralized location may need to be set up even when there are decentralized sites established.

- The location should include physically separated treatment areas and a morgue.
- Move survivors to the treatment area from where they were initially rescued, assessed, and treated. They should remain under treatment there until first responders can transport them to a location for professional medical treatment.
- A central medical treatment area facilitates the effective use of resources since a limited number of medical operation personnel in one location can take care of a greater number of survivors.
- First responders and other medical professionals will generally be able to transport the injured more efficiently from one central location than from multiple decentralized locations.
- Move the deceased to the morgue, which should be separated from the survivor treatment area, in the centralized treatment area.

Whether a treatment area is centralized or is one in several decentralized areas, the location(s) selected should be:

- Accessible by transportation vehicles (ambulances, trucks, helicopters, etc.); and
- Expandable.

Safety for Rescuers and Survivors

CERT volunteers may play a role in light search and rescue operations. Unit 7: Light Search and Rescue will cover this subject more in depth. As survivors are located, rescued, and assessed, they are moved to a location where medical personnel can treat them. As a reminder, the severity of the damage, number of injuries and casualties, and the safety of the immediate environment determine where the initial treatment area(s) should be located. In all cases, your individual safety is the number one priority.

- In structures with light damage, CERT members assess the survivors as they find them. Further medical treatment is performed in a safe location inside the designated treatment areas.
- In structures with moderate damage, CERT members assess the survivors as they find them; however, survivors are sent to a medical treatment area a safe distance from the incident.
- CERT members are not to enter a building with heavy damage under any circumstances.

CERT volunteers should never declare or attempt to move a patient who has died. If you find a deceased person (or a suspected deceased person), you should document the location and notify medical personnel.

SECTION 5: CONDUCTING HEAD-TO-TOE ASSESSMENTS

Conducting assessments and providing rapid treatment are the first steps CERT volunteers take when working with a patient.

During an assessment, you should look for:

- Severe bleeding;
- Low body temperature; and
- Airway obstruction.

A head-to-toe assessment goes beyond the immediate life-threatening injuries to try to determine the nature of the patient's injury. Perform the entire assessment before initiating treatment.

Do not conduct an assessment if a patient requires immediate care to prevent serious injury or death. In these cases, CERT volunteers should administer the necessary treatment before they follow up with an assessment.

Objectives of Head-to-Toe Assessments

The objectives of a head-to-toe assessment are to:

- Determine, as clearly as possible, the extent of injuries;
- Determine what type of treatment the patient needs; and
- Document injuries.

Remember to wear your PPE when conducting head-to-toe assessments.

What to Look for in Head-to-Toe Assessments

The medical community uses the acronym DCAP-BTLS to remember what to look for when conducting a rapid assessment. DCAP-BTLS stands for the following:

- Deformities;
- Contusions (bruising);
- Abrasions;
- Punctures;
- Burns;
- Tenderness;
- Lacerations; and
- Swelling.

When conducting a head-to-toe assessment, CERT volunteers should look for DCAP-BTLS in all parts of the body.

Remember to provide IMMEDIATE treatment for life-threatening injuries.

Pay careful attention to how people have been hurt (i.e., what caused the harm) because it provides insight to probable injuries suffered.

How to Conduct a Head-to-Toe Assessment

Whenever possible, CERT volunteers should ask the person about any injuries, pain, bleeding, or other symptoms. If the patient is conscious, CERT members should always ask permission to conduct the assessment. The patient has the right to refuse treatment.

Be sure to talk with the conscious patient to reduce anxiety.

Head-to-toe assessments should be:

- Conducted on all survivors, even those who seem all right;
- Verbal (if the patient is able to speak); and
- Hands-on. Do not be afraid to remove clothing to look.

Make sure you conduct each head-to-toe assessment the same way; doing so will make the procedure quicker and more accurate with each assessment. Remember to:

- Pay careful attention;
- Look, listen, and feel for anything unusual;
- Suspect a spinal injury in all unconscious survivors and treat accordingly; and
- Check your own hands for patient bleeding as you perform the head-to-toe assessment.

Check (DCAP-BTLS) body parts from the head to toe for fractured bones and soft tissue injuries in the following order:

1. Head;
2. Neck;
3. Shoulders;
4. Chest;
5. Arms;
6. Abdomen;
7. Pelvis; and
8. Legs.

While conducting a head-to-toe assessment, CERT volunteers should always check for:

- Pulse, Movement, Sensation (PMS) in all extremities; and
- Medical ID emblems on bracelet or necklace.

Closed-Head, Neck, and Spinal Injuries

When conducting head-to-toe assessments, rescuers may find survivors who have or may have suffered closed-head, neck, or spinal injuries.

A closed-head injury is a concussion-type injury as opposed to a laceration, or tear wound, although lacerations can indicate that the survivor has suffered a closed-head injury.

The main objective when CERT members encounter suspected injuries to the head or spine is to do no harm. You should minimize movement of the head and spine while treating any life-threatening conditions.

The signs of a closed-head, neck, or spinal injury most often include:

- Change in consciousness;
- Inability to move one or more body parts;
- Severe pain or pressure in head, neck, or back;
- Tingling or numbness in extremities;
- Difficulty breathing or seeing;
- Heavy bleeding, bruising, or deformity of the head or spine;
- Blood or fluid in the ears or nose;
- Bruising behind the ear;
- "Raccoon" eyes (bruising around eyes);
- "Uneven" pupils;
- Seizures; and
- Nausea or vomiting.

If survivors are exhibiting any of these signs or if the survivor is found under collapsed building material or heavy debris, you should treat them as having a closed-head, neck, or spinal injury.

Stabilizing the Head

During a disaster, ideal equipment is rarely available. CERT members may need to be creative by:

- Looking for materials — a door, desktop, building materials — to use as a backboard; and
- Looking for items — towels, draperies, or clothing — to stabilize the head on the board by tucking them snugly on either side of the head to immobilize it.

Only move survivors to increase the safety of the rescuer and survivor or when professional help will be delayed, and a medical treatment area is established to care for multiple survivors.

- Moving patients with suspected head, neck, or spinal injury requires sufficient patient stabilization. However, if the rescuer or patient is in immediate danger, safety is more important than any potential spinal injury and the rescuer should move the patient from the area as quickly as possible.

Unit 7: Light Search and Rescue will cover techniques for moving survivors.

Exercise 4.1: Conducting Head-to-Toe Assessments

Purpose: This exercise allows you to practice performing head-to-toe assessments on each other.

Complete this exercise as many times as possible with different "patients."

Instructions:

1. Break down into groups of two. One person will play the rescuer, the other person will be the patient.
2. The patients will lie on the floor on their backs and close their eyes.
3. The rescuers will conduct a head-to-toe assessment on the patients, following the procedure demonstrated earlier. The rescuer will then repeat the head-to-toe assessment.
4. After the rescuer has made at least two observed head-to-toe assessments, the patient and rescuer will change roles.
5. Each new rescuer will perform at least two head-to-toe assessments.

SECTION 6: PUBLIC HEALTH CONSIDERATIONS

When disaster survivors are sheltered together for treatment, public health becomes a concern. CERT members and CERT programs should take measures to avoid the spread of disease.

The primary public health measures include:

- Maintaining proper hygiene;
- Maintaining proper sanitation;
- Purifying water (if necessary); and
- Preventing the spread of disease.

Maintaining Hygiene

The maintenance of proper personal hygiene is critical even under makeshift conditions. Some steps individuals should take to maintain hygiene are listed below.

- Wash hands frequently using soap and water. Hand washing should be thorough (at least 15 to 20 seconds of vigorous rubbing on all surfaces of the hand). Alcohol-based hand sanitizers, which do not require water, are a good alternative to hand washing. The U.S. Centers for Disease Control (CDC) recommends products that are at least 60 percent alcohol. To use an alcohol-based hand sanitizer, apply about ½ teaspoon of the product to the palm of your hand. Rub your hands together, covering all surfaces, until hands are dry.
- Wear non-latex exam gloves at all times. Change or disinfect gloves after examining and/or treating each patient. Under field conditions, individuals can use rubber gloves if sterilized between treating survivors using bleach and water (one-part bleach to 10 parts water).
- Keep dressings sterile. Do not remove the wrapping from dressings until use. After opening, use the entire package of dressing, if possible.
- Wash any areas using soap and water or diluted bleach that come in contact with body fluids.

Practice proper hygiene techniques even during exercises.

Maintaining Sanitation

Poor sanitation is a major cause of infection. CERT medical operations personnel can maintain sanitary conditions by following some simple steps.

- Controlling the disposal of bacterial sources (e.g., soiled exam gloves, dressings).
- Putting waste products in plastic bags, tying off the bags, and marking them as medical waste. Keep medical waste separate from other trash and dispose of it as hazardous waste.
- Burying human waste. Select a burial site away from the operations area and mark the burial site for later cleanup.

Water Purification

Potable water supplies are often in short supply during a disaster. Purify water for drinking, cooking, and medical use by heating it to a rolling boil for 1 minute or by using water purification tablets or non-perfumed liquid bleach.

The bleach to water ratios are:

- 8 drops of bleach per gallon of water; and
- 16 drops per gallon if the water is cloudy or dirty.

Let the bleach and water solution stand for 30 minutes. Note, if the solution does not smell of bleach, add another six drops of bleach and let the solution stand for 15 minutes.

Rescuers should not put anything on wounds other than purified water. The use of other solutions (e.g., hydrogen peroxide) on wounds must be the decision of trained medical personnel.

UNIT 4 SUMMARY

The key points of this unit are:

- During a mass casualty incident, where the number of injured and dead overwhelms local resources, CERT volunteers should:
  - Identify yourself as a CERT volunteer and your local agency affiliation.
  - Assess the situation and provide life-saving interventions if a first responder is not available.
  - Provide responders with detailed information from your size-up when they arrive on scene.
  - Remember that communication is key for supporting first responders.
- Disaster medical operations include these major functions:
  - Triage/Assessment;
  - Treatment;
  - Transport;
  - Morgue; and
  - Supply.
- Treatment areas will take into consideration safety for rescuers and survivors and proximity to resources.
- Depending on the circumstances, a first responder may establish a central medical treatment location and/or treatment locations at multiple incident sites with many injured survivors.
- Head-to-toe assessments should be hands-on and verbal. Always conduct head-to-toe assessments in the same way—beginning with the head and moving toward the feet. If you suspect injuries to the head, neck, or spine, the main objective is to not cause additional injury. Use in-line stabilization and a backboard if you must move the survivor.
- To safeguard public health, take measures to maintain proper hygiene and sanitation, and purify water, if necessary. In advance, plan all public health measures and practice during exercises.

Homework Assignment

Read and become familiar with the unit to be covered in the next session.

Try practicing a rapid head-to-toe assessment on a friend or family member. Do not forget to document!

CERT Unit 5:
Disaster Psychology

Participant Manual

CERT Unit 5: Disaster Psychology

In this unit, you will learn about:

- **Disaster Psychology:** The psychological impact a disaster has on rescuers and survivors, and lessons on providing components of "psychological first aid."

- **Caring for Yourself and Survivors:** Steps volunteers can take individually and as part of a CERT before, following, and after a disaster.

CERT Unit 5 Table of Contents

SECTION 1: UNIT 5 OVERVIEW

CERT volunteers encounter things during a disaster that are unpleasant and uncomfortable. In responding to both natural disasters and acts of violence, CERT volunteers must be prepared to deal with the psychological effects of the trauma. These may include fear, anger, intense sadness, frustration, and traumatic grief. Survivors and CERT volunteers alike are at risk for experiencing these psychological effects.

CERT volunteers prepare themselves for their role during and following a disaster by learning about the possible emotional and physical impact of disasters on them and others. This knowledge helps CERT volunteers understand and manage their reactions to the event while enabling them to work better with others.

Remember what you have learned about team organization. Team organization concepts can help you both operationally and psychologically. Working together and looking out for each other are important aspects of successful teams.

Psychological first aid is not therapy; rather, it is a set of techniques to provide emotional intervention during field operations. The techniques covered in this unit will help you manage personal situations, so you can meet the needs of all survivors, including your fellow CERT volunteers.

Unit Objectives

At the end of this unit, you should be able to:

1. Understand disaster trauma for survivors and rescuers, including CERT volunteers.
2. List steps to take for personal and team well-being.
3. Demonstrate key steps to apply when providing aid to someone with survivor's trauma.

SECTION 2: DISASTER REACTIONS

During a disaster, you may encounter things that will be extremely unpleasant. Normal stress reactions to disaster environments can result from:

1. Dealing with your own personal losses;
2. Working in your neighborhood;
3. Assisting neighbors, friends, or coworkers who have been injured; and
4. Feeling unsafe and insecure.

"Vicarious trauma" is a common occupational hazard for disaster response volunteers. Vicarious trauma—also referred to as compassion fatigue, secondary victimization, or secondary traumatic stress—is a natural reaction of an individual exposed to a survivor's trauma. A person who identifies too strongly with a survivor may take on that survivor's feelings.

Taking on the survivors' feelings as your own can affect your ability to do your job as a rescuer and it can have long-term impact. Taking ownership of others' problems will compound your own stress and negatively affect your overall effectiveness.

Be alert to signs of disaster trauma in yourself, as well as in disaster survivors and others, such as fellow CERT volunteers, so you can take steps to alleviate stress. The term "burnout" is different from trauma. Typically, individuals suffering from burnout can overcome it by distancing themselves from their work for a period of time.

The Five Fs

Humans typically have five primary responses to stress. We refer to those as the 5 Fs: (1) freeze, (2) flight, (3) fight, (4) fright, and (5) faint. Our bodies have both physical and psychological responses to stressful events. Recognizing examples of each of these responses in both CERT volunteers and survivors can assist you in determining how best to provide support.

1. **Freeze:** "Stop, look, and listen," or be on guard and watchful.
2. **Flight:** Flee.
3. **Fight:** Attempt to combat the threat.
4. **Fright:** Tonic immobility when in contact with a predator or playing dead.
5. **Faint:** Fear-induced fainting.

Possible Psychological Symptoms

You may experience or observe others experience varied types of disaster-related psychological and physiological responses.

- **Emotional:** nervousness; helplessness; shock; numbness; inability to feel love or joy; feelings of abandonment; agitation; feelings of detachment; exhilaration as a result of surviving; unreal feelings; feelings of being out of control; instances of denial; feelings of being overwhelmed; and feelings of fragility.
- **Cognitive:** difficulty making decisions; occurrence of disturbing dreams; memories and flashbacks; feelings of always being on guard or on constant alert;

feelings of dissociation; distortion of time and space; rumination or racing thoughts; or repeatedly replaying the traumatic event.

- **Spiritual:** loss of hope; limited expectations about life, intense use of prayer; loss of self-efficacy; feelings of despair and disillusionment; questioning ("Why Me?"); redefining meaning and importance of life.

Possible Physical Symptoms

- Loss of appetite
- Headaches or chest pain
- Diarrhea, stomach pain, or nausea
- Hyperactivity
- Increase in alcohol or drug consumption
- Nightmares
- The inability to sleep
- Fatigue or low energy

SECTION 3: SELF-CARE AND TEAM WELL-BEING

There is a range of actions you can take before, during, and after an incident to help manage the emotional impact of disaster response work.

Knowing in advance the possible psychological and physiological symptoms of disaster trauma covered in this unit is one-step in managing the impact.

Some other aspects of stress management for CERT volunteers include actions that CERT volunteers can take for themselves and actions CERT leaders can take during a response.

Ways to Reduce Your Own Stress

Only you know how to reduce your stress levels. It is worthwhile to spend the time and effort to find personal stress reducers before an incident occurs.

You can take the following preventive steps in your everyday life.

- Get enough sleep.
- Exercise regularly.
- Eat a balanced diet.
- Balance work, play, and rest.
- Allow yourself to receive as well as give; you should remember that your identity is broader than that of a helper.
- Connect with others.
- Use spiritual resources.

In addition to preventive steps, you should explain to your loved ones and friends how to support you when you return from a disaster area.

- Listen when you want to talk.
- Do **not** force you to talk if you are not ready

You may also want to share with your loved ones and friends the information on possible disaster-related psychological and physiological symptoms discussed earlier.

Exercise 5.1: Self-Care Toolbox

Purpose: This activity is to provide you with the opportunity to outline a number of self-care tools that you can perform both before and during a crisis so that you are ready to respond during an emergency.

Instructions: Complete this activity individually and at your own pace. When everyone has finished, you will have the opportunity to share your responses with the class if you would like.

Image 5.1: Self-Care Toolkit (Part 1)

What is likely to be your greatest challenge?
List out in rank order, what kinds of events may
be most difficult for you. Examples of events
that are difficult for lots of people: events
involving pets, animals, children, or the elderly;
contagious disease, intentional human-to-
human harm.

What skills do you have that may come in
handy during a crisis?

How do you know that you are feeling
stressed? List symptoms that characterize you
when you are feeling stressed (e.g., thoughts,
feelings, body sensations, or behaviors).

Make a list of things that help you relax (e.g.,
listening to music, taking a walk, reading a
book, laughing, and talking with a loved one).

Make a list of things you need to avoid (and
that you would likely do without consideration)
that will only add to your stress (e.g., drinking
too much caffeine, overindulging in media,
sitting for the whole day/shift, and taking on
someone else's tasks).

We all need to talk about our experiences from
time to time. Who are the top five people you
can go talk to during or after a crisis?

What things can others do for you when you
are feeling stressed?

Image 5.1: Self-Care Toolkit (Part 1)

How can you tell others what you need? How will you tell them?

The following areas are daily things that we either do or do not do that affect our ability to respond to emergencies. Following each one, rank how well you do in that area (1 = very poor, 10 = excellent) and then write down one action you can take to improve that area by one point.

Nutrition | 1 | 2 | 3 | 4 | 5 | 6 | 7 | 8 | 9 | 10

What can you do:

Sleep | 1 | 2 | 3 | 4 | 5 | 6 | 7 | 8 | 9 | 10

What can you do:

Manage Workload | 1 | 2 | 3 | 4 | 5 | 6 | 7 | 8 | 9 | 10

What can you do:

Balanced Lifestyle | 1 | 2 | 3 | 4 | 5 | 6 | 7 | 8 | 9 | 10

What can you do:

Stress Management | 1 | 2 | 3 | 4 | 5 | 6 | 7 | 8 | 9 | 10

What can you do:

Having fun | 1 | 2 | 3 | 4 | 5 | 6 | 7 | 8 | 9 | 10

What can you do:

Social network | 1 | 2 | 3 | 4 | 5 | 6 | 7 | 8 | 9 | 10

What can you do:

Exercise (30 min/day) | 1 | 2 | 3 | 4 | 5 | 6 | 7 | 8 | 9 | 10

What can you do:

How Team Leaders Reduce Stress During the Incident

There are steps that CERT TLs can take to reduce the stress on rescue workers before, during, and after an incident.

- Brief CERT personnel before the effort begins on what they can expect to see and what they can expect in terms of emotional response in the survivors and themselves.
- Emphasize the team aspect of CERT. Sharing the workload and emotional load can help defuse pent-up emotions.
- Encourage rescuers to rest and regroup to avoid becoming overtired.
- Direct rescuers to take breaks away from the incident area for relief from the stress of the effort.
- Establish a culture of acceptance amongst the team. Encourage volunteers to verbalize their experiences and normalize open communication.
- Encourage rescuers to eat properly and maintain fluid intake during the operation. Encourage them to drink water or other electrolyte-replacing fluids, avoiding drinks with caffeine or refined sugar.
- Encourage volunteers to be aware of changes in their teammates that may indicate personal stress and the need for a break or change of assignment.
- Rotate teams for breaks or new duties (e.g., from high-stress to low-stress jobs). Encourage volunteers to talk with each other about their experiences to promote psychological health.
- Do **not** send home volunteers who just completed a high-stress operation; instead, assign them to a low-stress responsibility so they can decompress gradually.
- Conduct a brief discussion with rescue workers after their shift during which they can describe and express their feelings about what they encountered.

SECTION 4: WORKING WITH SURVIVORS' EMOTIONAL RESPONSES

Crisis survivors can go through a variety of emotional phases, and as a rescuer, you should be aware of what you may encounter. The conditions associated with evacuation and relocation have psychological significance. When there are physical hazards or family separations during the evacuation process, survivors often experience post-traumatic reactions. When the family unit is not together due to shelter requirements or other factors, anxiety regarding the welfare of those not present may detract from the attention necessary for immediate problem solving.

- **Pre-Disaster Phase:** Communities will have varying degrees of warning depending on the type of disaster. For example, earthquakes typically hit without warning; whereas, hurricanes and floods typically strike within hours to days of a warning. When there is no warning, survivors may feel more vulnerable, unsafe, and fearful of future unpredicted tragedies. The perception they had no control over protecting themselves or their loved ones can be deeply distressing. Meanwhile, when people do not heed warnings and suffer losses as a result, they may experience guilt and self-blame. While they may have specific plans for how they might protect themselves in the future, survivors often feel guilty or responsible for what has occurred.
- **Impact Phase:** The impact phase of a disaster varies from the slow, low threat buildup associated with some types of floods to the violent, dangerous, and destructive outcomes associated with tornadoes and explosions. The greater the scope, community destruction, and personal losses associated with the disaster, the greater the psychosocial effects.

  Depending on the characteristics of the incident, people's reactions may range from constricted, stunned, shock-like responses to the less common overt expressions of panic and hysteria. Typically, people respond initially with confusion and disbelief and focus on the survival and physical well-being of themselves and their loved ones. When families are in different geographic locations during the impact of a disaster (e.g., children at school, adults at work), survivors will experience considerable anxiety until reunification.
- **Heroic Phase:** In the immediate aftermath of a disaster, survival, rescuing others, and promoting safety are priorities. Evacuation to shelters, motels, or other homes may be necessary. For some, post-impact disorientation gives way to adrenaline-induced rescue behavior to save lives and protect property. While activity level may be high, actual productivity is often low. The capacity to assess risk may be impaired, and injuries can result. Altruism is prominent among both survivors and emergency responders.
- **Honeymoon Phase:** In the weeks and months following a disaster, formal governmental and volunteer assistance may be readily available. Community bonding occurs from the shared experience of surviving a catastrophic experience and the giving and receiving of community support. Survivors may experience a short-lived sense of optimism that the help they will receive will make them "whole" again. When disaster behavioral health workers are visible

and perceived as helpful during this phase, they are more readily accepted and have a foundation from which to aid in the difficult phases ahead.

- **Disillusionment Phase:** Disappointment in a slower-than-expected pace of recovery can trigger this phase. Disillusionment typically occurs in the second half of the year immediately following a disaster and, again, after the disaster's first anniversary.
- **Reconstruction Phase:** The reconstruction of physical property and recovery of emotional well-being may continue for years following a disaster. At this point, survivors have realized they will need to solve the problems of rebuilding their own homes, businesses, and lives largely by themselves and have gradually assumed the responsibility for doing so.

Traumatic Crisis

A traumatic crisis is an event experienced or witnessed in which people's ability to cope is overwhelmed by:

- Actual or potential death or injury to self or others;
- Serious injury;
- Destruction of their homes, neighborhood, or valued possessions; and/or
- Loss of contact with family volunteers or close friends.

Traumatic stress may affect:

- **Cognitive Function**: Those who have suffered traumatic stress may act irrationally, in ways out of character for them, and they may have difficulty making decisions. Additionally, they may have difficulty sharing or retrieving memories.
- **Physical Health**: Traumatic stress can cause physical symptoms and health problems.
- **Interpersonal Relationships**: Survivors of traumatic stress may undergo temporary or long-term personality changes that make interpersonal relationships difficult.

Mediating Factors

The strength and type of personal reaction to trauma vary depending on a combination of the following factors:

- A person's prior experience with the same or a similar event; the emotional effect of multiple events can be cumulative, leading to greater stress reactions.
- Intensity of the disruption in the survivors' lives; the more the survivors' lives are disrupted, the greater their psychological and physiological reactions may become.
- The meaning of the event to the individual; the more catastrophic the victim perceives the event to be to him or her personally, the more intense his or her stress reaction will be.

- The emotional well-being of the individual and the resources (especially social) that he or she has to cope. People who have had other recent traumas may not cope well with additional stresses.
- The length of time that has elapsed between the event's occurrence and the present; the reality of the event takes time to "sink in."

CERT volunteers cannot know—and should never assume to know—what someone is thinking or feeling.

Do not take the survivors' surface attitudes personally. Rescuers should expect to see a range of responses that will vary from person to person, but the responses they see will be part of the psychological impact of the event—and probably will not relate to anything that the CERTs have or have not done.

Stabilizing Survivors

The goal of on-scene psychological intervention on the part of CERT volunteers should be to calm the incident scene by stabilizing individuals. Address any medical needs then use the methods below to psychologically stabilize individuals.

- Observe survivors to determine their level of responsiveness and decide whether they pose a danger to themselves or to others.
- Get uninjured people involved in helping. Engaging survivors in focused activity helps them cope. Give them constructive jobs to do such as organizing supplies. This strategy is especially effective for survivors who are being disruptive.

Provide support by:

- **Listening:** Let them talk about their feelings and their physical needs. Survivors often need to talk about what they have been through – and they may want someone to listen to them.
- **Empathizing:** Caring responses show survivors that someone else shares their feelings of pain and grief.
- **Connecting:** Help survivors connect to natural support systems, such as family, friends, or clergy.

Listen, Protect, Connect

Psychological First Aid (PFA) is an evidence-informed approach to assist children, adolescents, adults, and families in a disaster's aftermath. Just as you learned basic first aid in Units 3 and 4 to support the physical needs of survivors, PFA provides the initial support for survivors' psychological well-being. "Listen, Protect, Connect" is one method of PFA that can assist survivors in taking steps to bounce back more quickly.

- **Listen**: The first important step to help your survivors after an event is to listen and pay attention to what they say (and how they say it), how they act, and what they need right now. We talked previously about the many ways in which people may react after experiencing a traumatic event. Remember that not all reactions are verbal or can be seen.

Let the survivor(s) know you are willing to listen and talk about the event when or if they would like to. Understand that sometimes survivors are not ready to talk or do not want to talk and that is okay. Check back with them on a regular basis to see if their reactions or needs have changed.

- **Protect:** This step helps survivors feel protected and allows you to protect them from added stress. This step helps survivors feel better by taking actions to provide support, encouragement, and reassurance. The listening step should have provided you with enough information to make informed decisions about each survivor's needs.
    - Provide information or resources.
    - Answer questions simply and honestly, clearing up any confusion they may have.
    - Empathize and let them know they are not alone in their reactions to the event.
    - Provide opportunities for them to communicate, but do not force them.
    - Talk to them about what is being done to keep everyone safe from harm.
    - Watch for anything in the environment that could re-traumatize them such as sights, smells, or sounds and help them reduce contact with those elements.
    - Help them decide what their basic needs are and how to get access to them (e.g., encouraging healthy behaviors such as food and rest).
- **Connect**: Connecting survivors to their friends, loved ones, and other resources has a positive impact on their recovery.
    - Assist survivors in reconnecting with friends or loved ones after a disaster.
    - Ensure you are connecting with them on a regular basis.
    - Help them find access to resources that can offer support.

Being an Empathetic Listener

Being an empathetic listener requires the listener to listen and to let the survivor talk.

Good listeners will:

- Put the listener in the speaker's shoes to understand the speaker's point of view more profoundly. Draw upon experiences or try to imagine how the speaker is feeling. To limit the effects of vicarious trauma, be careful not to completely take on the speaker's feelings.
- Listen for meaning, not just words, and pay close attention to the speaker's nonverbal communication, such as body language, facial expressions, and tone of voice.
- Paraphrase the speaker periodically to make sure he or she fully understood what the speaker said and to indicate to the speaker that you are listening. This reinforces the communication process.

Survivors can show evidence of being suicidal, psychotic, or unable to care for themselves. Be sure to refer these cases to EMS and/or mental health professionals for support as soon as possible.

What Not to Say

When providing support, you should avoid saying the following phrases. On the surface, you may say these phrases to comfort the survivors, but they can be misinterpreted or not well received. In general, avoid the statements below:

- "I understand." In most situations, we cannot understand unless we have had the same experience.
- "Don't feel bad." The survivor has a right to feel bad and will need time to feel differently.
- "You're strong" or "You'll get through this." Many survivors do not feel strong and question if they will recover from the loss.
- "Don't cry." It is okay to cry.
- "It's God's will." With a person you do not know, giving religious meaning to an event may insult or anger the person.
- "It could be worse," "At least you still have…", or "Everything will be okay." It is up to the individual to decide whether things could be worse or if everything will be okay.

Rather than provide comfort, these types of responses could elicit a strong negative response or distance the survivor from the listener.

It is okay to apologize if the survivor reacts negatively to something you said.

Learn to be comfortable with silence. Do not say something just to alleviate your own discomfort.

Say This Instead

Always ask permission to enter their space, provide help, or interact with them.

Allow people to say what they need. Normalize what they are feeling and thinking using common phrases similar to those below.

- "I'm sorry for your pain."
- "I'm so sorry this has happened."
- "Is it all right if I help you with…?"
- "I can't imagine what this is like for you."
- "What do you need?"

Managing Death Scene

One unpleasant task that CERT volunteers may face is dealing with a victim who dies while under the team's care. The guidelines below are useful for dealing with this situation.

- Cover the body; treat it with respect.
- Follow local laws and protocols for handling the deceased.
- Talk with local authorities to determine the plan.

UNIT 5 SUMMARY

The key points from this unit are:

- A disaster may expose rescuers to extremely unpleasant or uncomfortable situations. These experiences will be stressful and may be traumatic.
- Over-identifying with survivors may subject rescuers to vicarious trauma.
- Survivors and rescuers may have both psychological and physiological symptoms of trauma after a disaster.
- CERT leaders can take steps to reduce stress on rescue workers before, during, and after an incident.
- CERT volunteers can take steps to reduce stress on themselves.
- Psychological First Aid is an evidence-informed approach for assisting children, adolescents, adults, and families in the aftermath of disaster.
- The steps *listen, protect, and connect* can provide actions associated with supporting survivors after a disaster.
- Research shows that survivors go through the following distinct emotional phases following a disaster:
    - Pre-Disaster
    - Impact
    - Heroic
    - Honeymoon
    - Disillusionment
    - Reconstruction
- Traumatic stress may affect cognitive functioning, physical health, and interpersonal reactions.
- Different people react differently to traumatic stress based on a variety of mediating factors.
- A traumatic crisis occurs when a person's ability to cope is overwhelmed.
- The goal of on-scene psychological intervention is to stabilize the incident by stabilizing individuals.
- Provide support for survivors by being an empathetic listener.

Homework Assignment

Read and become familiarize yourself with the unit that will be covered in the next session.

CERT Unit 6:
Fire Safety and Utility
Controls

Participant Manual

CERT Unit 6: Fire Safety and Utility Controls

In this unit, you will learn about:

- **Fire Chemistry:** How fire occurs, classes of fire, and choosing the correct means to extinguish each type of fire.

- **Fire Size-up Considerations:** How to evaluate fires, assess firefighting resources and determine a course of action.

- **Portable Fire Extinguishers:** How to identify types of portable fire extinguishers and how to operate them.

- **Fire Suppression Safety:** How to decide if you should attempt to extinguish a fire; how to approach and extinguish a fire safely.

- **Hazardous Materials:** How to identify potentially dangerous materials in storage, in transit, and in your home.

- **Fire and Utility Hazards:** How to identify potential fire and utility hazards in the home and workplace; how to implement successful fire prevention strategies.

CERT Unit 6 Table of Contents

SECTION 1: UNIT 6 OVERVIEW

During, and immediately following a fire emergency, the first priorities of fire services are life safety, incident stabilization, and property conservation.

Limited access to roads, weather conditions, inadequate water supply, and limited resources may hamper and slow the response time of responders.

Unit Objectives

At the end of this unit, you should be able to:

1. Explain the role CERTs play in fire safety and response, including the CERT size-up process and minimum safety precautions.
2. Extinguish a small fire using a fire extinguisher.
3. Identify and reduce potential fire, utility, and hazardous materials hazards at home and in the community.

Role of CERTs

CERTs play a very important role in fire and utility safety by supporting the following actions.

- Extinguishing small fires before they become major fires.
  - This unit will provide training on how to use an extinguisher to put out small fires and how to recognize when a fire is too big to handle. As a rule, if you cannot put out a fire in five seconds, it is already too big to handle, and you should leave the premises immediately.
- Preventing additional fires by removing fuel sources.
  - This unit will describe how to perform an "overhaul," the process to ensure you extinguish a fire completely and permanently.
- Shutting off utilities when necessary and safe to do so.
  - This unit will review utility shutoff procedures taught in Unit 1.
- Assisting with evacuations where necessary.
  - When a fire is beyond the ability of CERTs to extinguish or a utility emergency has occurred, CERT volunteers need to protect lives by evacuating the area and establishing a perimeter, while also notifying fire services of the situation.

CERT Priorities

CERTs play a very important role in neighborhood and workplace fire and utility safety. CERT volunteers help in fire- and utility-related emergencies before professional responders arrive. When responding, CERT volunteers should keep in mind the following CERT standards:

Rescuer safety is always the number one priority. Therefore, CERT volunteers should always:

- Use the buddy system. Buddies serve an important purpose. They protect your safety. Do not ever try to fight a fire alone. Stick together at all times.

- Wear safety equipment (gloves, helmet, goggles, N95 mask, and sturdy shoes or boots). Unless otherwise stated, this equipment is generally not fire-resistant PPE.
- The CERT goal is to do the greatest good for the greatest number.

SECTION 2: FIRE CHEMISTRY

The Fire Triangle

Fire requires three elements to exist:

- **Heat:** Heat is required to elevate the temperature of a material to its ignition point.
- **Fuel:** The fuel for a fire may be a solid, liquid, or gas. The type and quantity of the fuel will determine which method you should use to extinguish the fire.
- **Oxygen:** Most fires will burn vigorously in any atmosphere of at least 20 percent oxygen. Without oxygen, most fuels could be heated until entirely consumed yet they would not burn.

These three elements, called the fire triangle, create a chemical exothermic reaction, which is fire.

Image 6.1: Fire Triangle

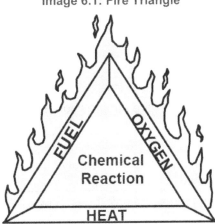

Classes of Fires

To aid in distinguishing types of fires, fires are categorized into classes based on the type of fuel that is burning.

- **Class A Fires:** Ordinary combustibles, such as paper, cloth, wood, rubber, and many plastics.
- **Class B Fires:** Flammable liquids, including oils and gasoline as well as combustible liquids such as charcoal lighter fluid and kerosene. Only the vapor burns when ignited.
- **Class C Fires:** Energized electrical equipment, such as wires and motors. When the electricity is turned off, the fire becomes a Class A fire.
- **Class D Fires:** Combustible metals, including aluminum, magnesium, and titanium.
- **Class K Fires:** Cooking oils, such as vegetable oils, animal oils, and fats.

It is extremely important to identify the type of fuel feeding the fire in order to select the correct method and agent for extinguishing the fire.

SECTION 3: FIRE SIZE-UP CONSIDERATIONS

As introduced in Unit 2, size-up is a continual process that enables professional responders to make decisions and respond appropriately in the areas of greatest need. CERT size-up consists of nine steps and should be used in any emergency, including during fire situations.

Size-up of a situation involving a fire will dictate whether to attempt fire suppression and will help you plan for extinguishing the fire.

The safety of individual CERT volunteers is always the top priority. An effective fire size-up will allow participants to answer all of the following questions:

- Do my buddy and I have the right equipment?
- Are there other hazards?
- Is the building structurally damaged?
- Can my buddy and I escape?
- Can my buddy and I fight the fire safely?

Table 6.1: CERT Fire Size-up

Step 1: Gather Facts		
Time		
Does the time of day or week affect fire suppression efforts? How?	Yes	No
Weather		
Are there weather conditions that affect your safety? If yes, how will your safety be affected?	Yes	No
Will weather conditions affect the situation? If yes, how will the situation be affected?	Yes	No
Type of Construction		
What type(s) of structure(s) is (are) involved?		
What type(s) of construction is (are) involved?		
Occupancy		
Are the structures occupied? If yes, how many people are likely to be affected?	Yes	No
Are there special considerations (e.g. children, elderly, pets, people with access and functional needs)?	Yes	No
Hazards		
Are hazardous materials evident?	Yes	No
Are any other types of hazards involved? Is yes, what other hazards?	Yes	No

Step 2: Assess and Communicate the Damage		
Survey all sides of the scene. Is the danger beyond the CERT's capability?	Yes	No
Have the facts and the initial damage assessment been communicated to the appropriate person(s)?	Yes	No
Step 3: Consider Possibilities		
Life Hazards		
Are there potentially life-threatening hazards? If yes, what are the hazards?	Yes	No
Path of Fire		
Does the path of the fire jeopardize other areas? If yes, what other areas may be in jeopardy?	Yes	No
Additional Damage		
Is there a high potential for more disaster activity that will impact personal safety? If yes, what are the known risks?	Yes	No
Step 4: Assess Your Own Situation		
What equipment is available to help suppress the fire?		
What other resources are available?		
Can CERT volunteers *safely* attempt to suppress the fire? *If not, do not attempt suppression*.	Yes	No
Step 5: Establish Priorities		
Are there any other more pressing needs now? If yes, list.	Yes	No
Step 6: Make Decisions		
Where will resources do the most good while maintaining an adequate margin of safety?		
Step 7: Develop Plan of Action		
Determine how personnel and other resources should be used.		
Step 8: Take Action		
Put the plan into effect.		
Step 9: Evaluate Progress		
Continually size up the situation to identify changes in the scope of the problem, safety risks, and resources availability.		
Adjust strategies as required.		

Size-up is a continuous process. Evaluation of progress—Step 9—may require you to go back and gather additional facts.

SECTION 4: FIREFIGHTING RESOURCES

The most common firefighting resources are:

- Local fire departments;
- Fire alarm systems;
- Sprinkler systems;
- Portable fire extinguishers; and
- Interior wet standpipes (water hoses found in commercial or residential buildings, not for public use).

Fire Extinguishers

Portable fire extinguishers are invaluable for putting out small fires. A well-prepared home should have multiple portable fire extinguishers (locations could include kitchen, garage, workshop space, and basements). Workplaces are governed by regulation or fire code and should have the appropriate number of fire extinguishers as defined by regulation or fire code.

Keep in mind that the type of fuel that is burning will determine which resources to select to fight a fire.

Types of Fire Extinguishers

There are four types of extinguishers:

1. Water;
2. Dry chemical;
3. Carbon dioxide; and
4. Specialized.

Table 6.2: Fire Types, Extinguishing Agents, and Methods

Fire Type	Extinguishing Agent	Extinguishing Method
Ordinary Solid Materials	• Water • Foam • Dry chemical	• Removes heat • Removes air and heat • Breaks chain reaction
Flammable Liquids	• Foam • CO2 • Dry chemical	• Removes air • Breaks chain reaction
Electrical Equipment	• CO2 • Dry chemical	• Removes air • Breaks chain reaction

Fire Type	Extinguishing Agent	Extinguishing Method
Combustible Metals	• Special agents	• Usually removes air
Kitchen Oils	• Chemical	• Usually removes air

Extinguisher Rating and Labeling

The State Fire Marshal and Underwriters Laboratories (an organization that sets safety standards for manufactured goods) rates and approves all portable fire extinguishers. Extinguishers are rated according to their effectiveness on the different classes of fire. Manufacturers must label the strength and capability for each extinguisher, as well.

The label contains vital information about the type(s) of fire for which the extinguisher is appropriate. Extinguishers appropriate for Class A fires have a rating from 1A to 40A, with a higher number indicating a higher volume of extinguishing agent. Extinguishers appropriate for Class B fires have a rating from 1B to 640B. No number accompanies an extinguisher rated Class C, D, or K. The C on the label indicates only that the extinguisher is safe to use on electrical fires. Manufacturers label extinguishers for Class D fires to match the type of metal that is burning and with a list detailing the metals that match the unit's extinguishing agent. The extinguishers for Class K fires supplement fire suppression systems in commercial kitchens. They spray an alkaline mixture that, when combined with the fatty acid of the burning cooking oil or fat, creates soapy foam to hold in the vapors and extinguish the fire.

Image 6.2: Manufacturer's Label Illustration

UNDERWRITERS LABORATORIES INC. ®

DRY CHEMICAL FIRE EXTINGUISHER
CLASSIFICATION 3A:40B:C
TESTED IN ACCORDANCE WITH
ANSI/UL 711 AND ANSI/UL 299

NO.

MARINE TYPE U.S.C.G. TYPE A SIZE II TYPE B:C SIZE I
U.S.C.G. APPROVAL NO. 162.028/EX-2480
VALID ONLY WITH BRACKET NO. A-6

Sample manufacturer's label for a fire extinguisher, showing the Underwriters Laboratories symbol at the top, the type and classification of fire extinguisher, testing procedures used, and serial number. At the bottom of the label is marine information, including the U.S. Coast Guard approval number.

Water Extinguishers

Common characteristics of water extinguishers include:

- **Capacity:** Standard size is 2.5 gallons.
- **Range:** Standard range is 30-40 feet.
- **Pressure:** Standard pressure is 110 pounds per square inch (psi).

Use extreme caution when using a water extinguisher to ensure the water, which is under pressure, does not scatter lightweight materials and spread the fire.

Chemical Extinguishers

Dry chemical extinguishers are most common.

- Dry chemical extinguishers have a sodium bicarbonate base and are effective on Class B and C fires.
- Multipurpose dry chemical extinguishers have a monoammonium phosphate base and are effective for Class A, B, and C fires.

Common characteristics of dry chemical extinguishers include:

- **Capacity:** Approximately 10-20 seconds discharge time
- **Range:** Standard range is 8-12 feet.
- **Pressure:** Standard pressure is 175-250 psi.

While still in use, carbon dioxide and other specialized extinguishers are becoming less common.

Deciding to Use a Fire Extinguisher

There is a series of questions to ask before attempting to fight a fire with a fire extinguisher:

- Are there two ways to exit the area quickly and safely if I attempt to extinguish the fire?
- Do I have the right type of extinguisher for the type of fire?
- Is the extinguisher large enough for the fire?
- Is the area free from other dangers, such as hazardous materials and falling debris?
- Am I experienced or trained in the use of a fire extinguisher?

If you answer "NO" to any of these questions or if you have been unable to put out the fire in five seconds using the extinguisher, you should:

- Leave the building immediately (activate fire alarm system if it is safe to do so);
- While leaving, shut all doors to slow the spread of the fire; and
- Contact local fire department.

If you answer "YES" to all of these questions, you may attempt to extinguish the fire. Even if you answer "YES" to all of the questions but feel unable to extinguish the fire, you should leave immediately. You should always remember the five-second rule.

If the fire is extinguished in five seconds and the area is safe, you should stay and overhaul the fire. Overhauling is the process of searching a fire scene for hidden fire or sparks in an effort to prevent the fire from rekindling. Remember "cool, soak, and separate."

It is always a good idea to contact your local fire department even if you were able to extinguish a small fire. Fire department personnel will be able to assist with properly overhauling and ensuring that you extinguished the fire completely. In addition, insurance companies or workplace management (depending on your location) may want a report to have on file regarding the incident, especially if there is any damage.

Image 6.3: Deciding to Use a Fire Extinguisher

Can I escape quickly and safely from the area if I attempt to extinguish the fire and do not succeed?	NO →	LEAVE IMMEDIATELY!
YES ⬇		
Do I have the right type of extinguisher?	NO →	LEAVE IMMEDIATELY!
YES ⬇		
Is the extinguisher large enough for the fire?	NO →	LEAVE IMMEDIATELY!
YES ⬇		
Is the area free from the other dangers such as hazardous materials and falling debris?	NO →	LEAVE IMMEDIATELY!
YES ⬇		

START TO EXTINGUISH THE FIRE

Is the fire extinguished in five seconds?	NO →	LEAVE IMMEDIATELY!

YES ⬇

STAY AND OVERHAUL THE FIRE IF THE AREA IS SAFE

Image 6.4: Components of a Portable Fire Extinguisher

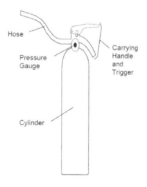

Hose
Pressure Gauge
Carrying Handle and Trigger
Cylinder

Components of a portable fire extinguisher: hose, carrying handle and trigger, pressure gauge, and cylinder.

P.A.S.S.

The acronym for operating a fire extinguisher is P.A.S.S.:

- Pull (Test the extinguisher after pulling the pin.);
- Aim;
- Squeeze; and
- Sweep.

To ensure the extinguisher is working properly, test it before approaching any fire.

Be sure to aim at the base of the fire; it is important to extinguish the fuel, not the flames.

Any fire extinguishers that have been completely depleted should be laid down and stored on their side so no attempt will be made to use them until they are recharged.

Image 6.5: P.A.S.S.

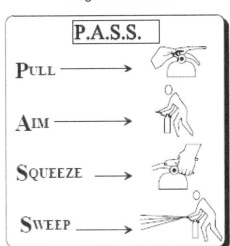

Interior Wet Standpipes

Interior wet standpipes are usually in commercial and apartment buildings and consist of 100 feet of 1.5-inch jacketed hose with an adjustable spray nozzle. They deliver at least 100 gallons of water per minute. Because of the size of the hose and the volume of water discharged, interior wet sandpipes can be difficult to manage. Therefore, CERT volunteers should never operate interior wet standpipes.

Confinement

In interior spaces, it is possible to confine a fire and restrict the spread of smoke and heat by closing interior and exterior doors.

SECTION 5: FIRE SUPPRESSION SAFETY

Small fire suppression may be one of your roles as a CERT volunteer. Your personal safety must always be your number one concern. You will be unable to help anyone if you have injured yourself through careless size-up or unsafe acts.

Fire Suppression Safety Rules

Volunteers should follow all rules regarding fire suppression safety.

- Use safety equipment at all times. Wear your helmet, goggles, dust mask, leather gloves, and sturdy shoes or boots. If you are not equipped to protect your personal safety, **leave the building**.
- Work with a buddy. Buddies serve an important purpose. They protect your safety. Do not ever try to fight a fire alone. Stick together at all times.
- Have a backup team, whenever possible. A backup team can support your fire suppression efforts and can provide help if you need it.
- Always have two ways to exit the fire area. Fires spread much faster than you might think. Always have a backup escape plan in case your main escape route becomes blocked.
- Look at the door. If air is being sucked under the door or smoke is seeping out the top of the door, do **not** touch or open the door.
- Feel closed doors with the back of the hand, working from the bottom of the door up including the space between the door and its frame. Do **not** touch the door handle before feeling the door. If the door is hot, there is fire behind it. Do **not** enter! Opening the door will feed additional oxygen to the fire.
- Confine the fire, whenever possible, by closing doors and keeping them closed.
- Stay low to the ground. Smoke inhalation is the leading cause of fire-related deaths. Smoke will naturally rise and keeping low to the ground will provide you with fresher air to breathe.
- Maintain a safe distance. Remember the effective range of your fire extinguisher. Do **not** get closer than necessary to extinguish the fire.
- Never turn your back on a fire when backing out.
- Overhaul the fire to be sure that it is extinguished—and stays extinguished.

Sometimes, what CERTs should not do when suppressing fires is just as important as what they should do.

- **DO NOT** get too close. Stay near the outer range of your extinguisher. If you feel the heat, you are too close.
- **DO NOT** try to fight a fire alone. Remember your first priority is your personal safety. Do **not** put it at risk.
- **DO NOT** try to suppress large fires. Learn the capability of your equipment, and do not try to suppress a fire that is clearly too large for the equipment at hand (e.g., a fire that is larger than the combined ratings of available fire extinguishers).
- **DO NOT** enter smoke-filled areas. Suppressing fires in smoke-filled areas requires equipment that CERTs do not have.

Proper Fire Suppression Procedures

Remember: CERT volunteers should use the buddy system in all cases. The job of Team Member 1 is to put out a fire with an extinguisher. Meanwhile, the job of Team Member 2 is to watch for hazards and ensure the safety of both team members. The six-step procedure for proper fire suppression is outlined below.

1. Assume ready position. With the pin pulled, Team Member 1 holds the extinguisher aimed and upright, approximately 20 to 25 feet from the fire for small fires.
2. When ready to approach the fire, Team Member 1 should say, "Ready." Team Member 2 should repeat, "Ready."
3. As Team Member 1 begins to move forward, he or she should say, "Going in." Team Member 2 should repeat the command and stay within reach of Team Member 1.
4. Both team members should walk toward the fire. Team Member 1 should watch the fire and Team Member 2 should stay close to Team Member 1, keeping his or her hand on Team Member 1's shoulder. Team Member 2's job is to protect Team Member 1.
5. When Team Member 1 is exiting the fire area, he or she should say, "Backing out." Team Member 2 should repeat the command.
6. Team Member 2 should guide Team Member 1 from the area with his or her hands as Team Member 1 continues facing the fire and looking for other hazards. Team Member 1 must never turn his or her back on the fire scene.

SECTION 6: FIRE AND UTILITY HAZARDS

This section will deal with identifying and preventing fire and utility hazards in the home and workplace.

Each of us has some type of fire or utility hazard in our home and workplace. Most of these hazards fall into the following categories:

- Electrical hazards;
- Natural gas hazards; or
- Flammable or combustible liquids.

Homes and workplaces can and do have other hazards, including incompatible materials stored in close proximity to each other, such as flammables/combustibles, corrosives, compressed gases, and explosives. Simple fire prevention measures will help reduce the likelihood of fires:

- First, locate potential sources of ignition; then
- Do what you can to reduce or eliminate the hazards.

Electrical Hazards

Here are some examples of common electrical hazards and simple ways CERT volunteers can reduce or eliminate them, such as:

- Avoid the "electrical octopus." Eliminate tangles of electrical cords.
- Do **not** overload electrical outlets.
- Do **not** plug power strips into other power strips.
- Do **not** run electrical cords under carpets.
- Check for and replace broken or frayed cords
- Maintain electrical appliances. Repair or replace malfunctioning appliances.

Responding to Electrical Emergencies

Electrical emergencies sometimes occur despite our best efforts. In the event of an electrical emergency, first responders, and even knowledgeable members of the household can take the following steps:

- Locate the circuit breakers or fuses and know how to shut off the power. Post shutoff instructions next to the breaker box or fuse box.
- Unscrew individual fuses or switch off smaller breakers first, then pull the main switch or breaker.
- When turning the power back on, turn on the main switch or breaker first, then screw in the fuses or switch on the smaller breakers, one at a time.

Be certain to notify a licensed electrician and/or utility company in the event of an electrical emergency or fire.

You should not enter a flooded basement or wade into standing water to shut off the electrical supply because water conducts electricity.

Image 6.6: Circuit Box and Fuse Box

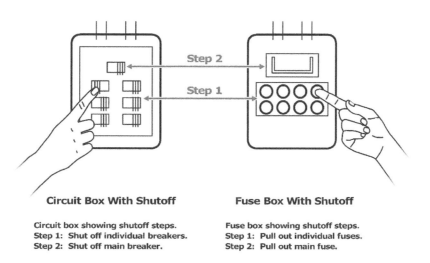

Circuit Box With Shutoff   **Fuse Box With Shutoff**

Circuit box showing shutoff steps.   Fuse box showing shutoff steps.
Step 1: Shut off individual breakers.   Step 1: Pull out individual fuses.
Step 2: Shut off main breaker.   Step 2: Pull out main fuse.

Natural Gas Hazards

Natural gas presents two types of hazards. It is an asphyxiant, which displaces oxygen in the body, and it is flammable meaning it can readily ignite under the right conditions

It is important to recognize that natural gas is lighter than air, and to understand that you will likely not be able to feel the gas in the event of a leak. Therefore, you should place natural gas detectors as you would smoke alarms, strategically on every level of your home. Common places to place natural gas detectors are near the furnace, hot water tank, and other gas appliances such as a clothes dryer or stove. Test the detector monthly to ensure it works.

Carbon Monoxide

Carbon monoxide (CO) is a deadly, colorless, odorless, poisonous gas that, like natural gas, is lighter than air. The incomplete burning of various fuels, including natural gas, is responsible for producing CO. Malfunctioning fuel-burning appliances such as furnaces, ranges, water heaters and room heaters; engine-powered equipment such as portable generators; fireplaces; and charcoal that is burned in homes and other enclosed areas are at risk for producing CO.

To prevent CO poisoning, install carbon monoxide detectors, which meet the current safety standards near all separate sleeping areas. You should install additional detectors on every level of the home and in every bedroom. Do not place detectors within 15 feet of heating or cooking appliances or in or near very humid areas such as bathrooms. Test the detector monthly to ensure it works.

Natural Gas Shutoff

Locate and clearly label the gas shutoff valve(s). There may be multiple valves inside a home in addition to the main shutoff. Know how to shut off the gas and have the proper non-sparking tool for shutting off the gas. If you are unsure of how to shut off the gas properly and safely, you should never attempt to do so. Contact your local gas company for assistance.

Image 6.7: Natural Gas Meter with Shutoff

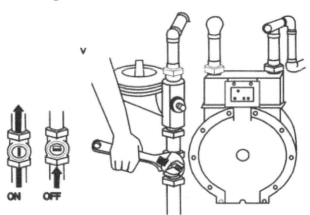

ON   OFF

The gas meter shutoff diagram indicates the shutoff valve location on the pipe that comes out of the ground. To turn off the valve, use a non-sparking wrench to turn the valve clockwise one-quarter turn. Remember that, in all cases, only a licensed technician should turn on natural gas flow.

Please note: Some gas meters have automatic shutoff valves that restrict the flow of gas during an earthquake or other emergency. A licensed plumber installs these, downstream of the utility point of delivery. If you are unsure whether your home has this shutoff device, contact your gas service company. If this shutoff device is closed, only a qualified professional should restore it.

Gas Meter Inside the Home

If your gas meter is located inside your home, you should only shut off the gas flow when instructed to by local authorities. If you smell gas or see the dials on your meter showing gas is flowing even though your appliances are off, you should evacuate the premises and call 9-1-1. Do not attempt to shut off the gas from inside the building if gas may be in the air.

Gas Meter Outside the Home

You should turn off the meter from outside the building if you smell gas or you see dials on the meter showing gas is flowing even though appliances are off. If there is a fire you cannot extinguish, call 9-1-1 and turn off the gas only if it is safe to do so.

Never enter the basement of a structure that is on fire to turn off any utility. Be sure to use a flashlight, not a candle, if you need additional light to locate and shut off the gas valve.

If you are unsure of the proper procedures, do not attempt to turn the utilities on again yourself, particularly in multiple-unit dwellings. Always follow your local fire department's guidelines. Remember that, in all cases, after the natural gas has been shut off, only a trained technician can restore it. Inappropriate or abrupt engagement of gas service may cause gas leaks inside the house.

Flammable Liquid Hazards

Tips for reducing hazards from flammable liquids:

- Read labels to identify flammable products; and
- Store them properly, using the L.I.E.S. method (Limit, Isolate, Eliminate, Separate).

If you need to use a fire extinguisher, you should only extinguish a flammable liquid using a portable fire extinguisher rated for Class B fires.

SECTION 7: HAZARDOUS MATERIALS

Materials are considered hazardous if they have **any** of these characteristics:

- Corrode other materials;
- Explode or are easily ignited;
- React strongly with water;
- Are unstable when exposed to heat or shock; and
- Are otherwise toxic to humans, animals, or the environment through absorption, inhalation, injection, or ingestion.

Hazardous materials include, but are not limited to:

- Explosives;
- Flammable gases and liquids;
- Poisons and poisonous gases;
- Corrosives;
- Nonflammable gases;
- Oxidizers; and
- Radioactive materials.

Identifying Hazardous Materials Locations

There are several ways to identify locations where hazardous materials are stored, used, or in transit.

- Location and type of occupancy;
- Placards and labels; and
- Sights, sounds, and smells.

Location and Type of Occupancy

Hazardous materials are commonplace throughout every community. Many commercial processes rely on hazardous materials and many retail outlets sell them. Despite protections in place, accidents and disasters can occur, causing these materials to release into the environment. Common locations in the community can include:

- Industrial locations, such as a warehouse, rail yard, or shipyard;
- Household locations, including under kitchen/bathroom sinks, workshop cabinets, garages, basements;
- Dry cleaner;
- Funeral home;
- Home supply store;
- Big box store; and
- Delivery van, such as overnight delivery services.

Placards

Warning placards are required whenever large amounts of hazardous materials are being stored, used, or transported. These placards act as an immediate warning system for emergency responders, helping them identify the kinds of materials present and the dangers they pose.

CERT volunteers should consider these placards a "stop sign."

National Fire Protection Association

The National Fire Protection Association (NFPA) 704 Diamond is a concise system for identifying the hazards associated with specific materials. CERT volunteers will find the NFPA 704 Diamond placard on fixed facilities where hazardous materials are used or stored.

The diamond is divided into four colored quadrants, each with a rating number inside of it, which indicates the degree of risk associated with the material. Numbers range from 0 to 4. **The higher the number the higher the risk!**

Image 6.8: NFPA 704 Diamond

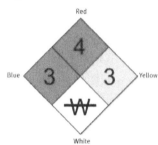

- The <u>red</u> quadrant describes the material's <u>flammability</u>.
- The <u>blue</u> quadrant indicates <u>health hazard</u>.
- The <u>yellow</u> quadrant indicates <u>reactivity</u>.
- The <u>white</u> quadrant indicates <u>special precautions</u>.

There are two symbols specified in the National Fire Codes, section 704.

- W indicates a material that displays unusual reactivity with water (e.g., should never be mixed with water or have water sprayed on it). Magnesium metal is an example of a material that is reactive to water.
- OX indicates a material that possesses oxidizing properties. Ammonium nitrate is an example of a material with oxidizing properties. Materials that are oxidizers increase the potential for explosion or fire.

In addition to the above symbols that are specified under the National Fire Codes, some NFPA 704 Diamonds will include additional symbols:

- ACID indicates that the material is an acid.
- ALK indicates that the material is a base.
- COR indicates that the material is corrosive.
- ☢ indicates that the material is radioactive.

The numbers within the NFPA 704 Diamond are used to assist professional firefighters in responding to accidents or fires.

The only action CERT volunteers should take is to evacuate persons who are downwind, as necessary, to an uphill or upwind location. Do not enter the building to evacuate people inside.

Global Harmonized System

The Globally Harmonized System of Classification and Labeling of Chemicals (GHS) is a system developed by the United Nations as a voluntary international system for chemical hazard communication. The GHS includes methods for classifying all hazardous chemical substances and mixtures.

There are three standard elements to a GHS safety label.

- Symbols use pictograms to communicate physical, health, and environmental hazard information.
- Signal Words indicate the severity of the hazard. "Danger" is used for severe hazards and "Warning" is used for less severe hazards. For lower level hazards, a signal word is not used.
- Hazard Statements are standardized phrases that describe each hazard presented by a chemical substance or mixture.

Image 6.9: GHS Pictograms

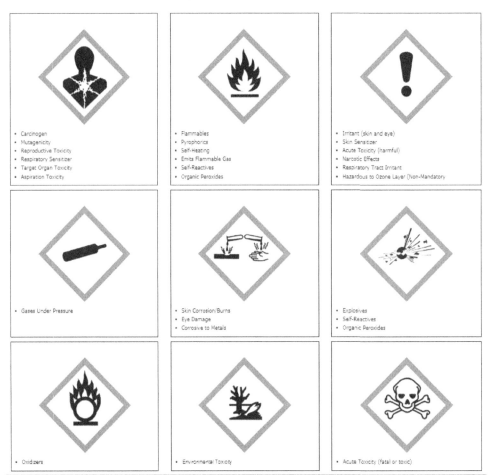

GHS labels also include the following additional elements:

- Precautionary Statements and Pictograms provide information to minimize or prevent the effects from a hazard;
- Product Identifiers, or the name or number used on a product's safety data sheet;
- Supplier Identification includes the name, address, and telephone number of the product's manufacturer or supplier; and
- Supplemental Information is additional, non-harmonized information that is not required or specified under the GHS.

Identifying Hazardous Materials in Transit

There are three ways that hazardous materials are marked and identified while in transit:

1. The Department of Transportation (DOT) placard;
2. The United Nations (UN) system; and
3. The North American (NA) warning placards.

These placards can be on any vehicle, not only tankers. Like the NFPA 704 Diamond, the DOT, UN, and NA placards should be a "stop sign" for CERT volunteers. You should always err on the side of safety. You should not assume that, because there is no placard, no hazardous materials are present. Treat any unknown situation as a hazardous materials incident.

- No placard is required for less than 1,000 pounds of many hazardous materials.
- Certain hazardous materials (e.g., anhydrous ammonia) are placarded as a nonflammable gas for domestic transport but as a flammable gas for international transport. (Anhydrous ammonia is a flammable gas!)
- Sometimes drivers forget to change the placard when they change their cargo. CERT volunteers should use extreme caution when approaching any vehicle in an accident.

Image 6.10: DOT Placard Warning

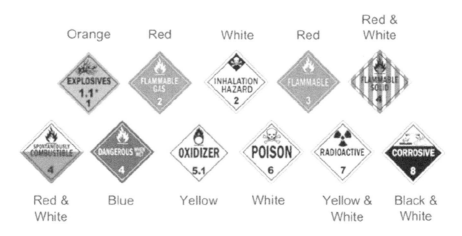

Emergency Response Guidebook

First responders use the Emergency Response Guidebook (ERG) for a transportation (e.g., highway or railway) emergency involving hazardous materials. The guide provides responders with information on how to identify the hazards quickly, and details how to protect themselves and the public from issues related to the hazards. Also included in the guide are the recommended evacuation distances for common hazards.

Sights, Sounds, and Smells

Hazardous materials are all around us and may be present regardless of the location or whether there are placards or other posted warnings. While hazardous materials often smell, sound, or look unusual, you may not be able recognize something toxic. Stay away from any unidentifiable substance and alert building managers or authorities.

Exercise 6.1: Suppressing Small Fires

Purpose: This exercise will provide you with experience in two key areas of fire suppression:

1. Using a portable fire extinguisher to suppress a small fire; and
2. Applying teamwork to fire suppression.

Instructions: Follow the steps below to conduct this exercise.

1. Identify possible exit routes, wind direction, and whether the fire is spreading.
2. When ready to approach the fire, Team Member 1 should say, "Ready." Team Member 2 should repeat, "Ready." As Team Member 1 begins to move forward, he or she should say, "Going in." Team Member 2 should repeat the command and place his or her hand on Team Member 1's shoulder and stay within reach of Team Member 1.
3. Both team members should walk toward the fire. Team Member 1 should watch the fire and Team Member 2 should stay close to Team Member 1, keeping his or her hand on Team Member 1's shoulder. Team Member 2's job is to protect Team Member 1.
4. Team Member 1 should approach the fire from the windward side (i.e., with the wind to the team member's back). When approximately 10 feet from the fire, Team Member 1 should begin to discharge the extinguisher at the base of the fire, continuing the approach until the range for the extinguisher is optimal.
5. Team Member 1 should sweep the base of the fire until it is extinguished.
6. . When Team Member 1 is ready to exit the fire area, he or she should say, "Backing out." Team Member 2 should repeat the command. Team Member 2 should guide Team Member 1 from the area with his or her hands as Team Member 1 continues facing the fire and looking for other hazards.

UNIT 6 SUMMARY

The key points of this unit are:

- Effective fire suppression depends on an understanding of:
  - The elements required for fire to exist;
  - The type of fuel involved;
  - The class of fire;
  - The resources required and available to extinguish each type of fire; and
  - Effective fire suppression techniques.
- Fire requires heat, fuel, and oxygen to exist.
- There are five types, or classes, of fire:
  - Class A: Ordinary combustibles;
  - Class B: Flammable liquids;
  - Class C: Energized electrical equipment;
  - Class D: Combustible metals; and
  - Class K: Cooking oils in commercial kitchens and cafeterias.
- It is extremely important to identify the class of fire to use the proper extinguisher for the class.
- Portable fire extinguishers are most frequently used to suppress small fires. Their labels tell the types of fires for which they are effective and the area that they can suppress.
- When using portable fire extinguishers, remember P.A.S.S.: Pull, Aim, Squeeze, and Sweep. Always test the extinguisher after pulling the pin.
- When suppressing a fire, always follow the safety rules established for CERTs.
- There are several methods of placarding hazardous materials being stored or transported, including NFPA, DOT, UN, and NA placards, to help volunteers understand the types of materials found at a specific location. When faced with accidents involving hazardous or unknown materials, volunteers should keep away and call for professional help immediately.

Homework Assignment

Before the next session, you should:

Read and familiarize yourself with the unit that will be covered in the next session.

CERT Unit 7:
Light Search and Rescue Operations

Participant Manual

CERT Unit 7: Light Search and Rescue Operations

In this unit, you will learn about:

☐ **Search and Rescue Size-up:** How to size up the situation in which the search and rescue teams will operate.

☐ **Conducting Interior and Exterior Search Operations:** How to search systematically for disaster survivors.

☐ **Conducting Rescue Operations:** Safe techniques for lifting, leveraging, cribbing, and survivor removal.

CERT Unit 7 Table of Contents

SECTION 1: UNIT 7 OVERVIEW

Unit Objectives

At the end of this unit, you should be able to:

1. Identify and apply CERT size-up requirements for potential search and rescue situations;
2. Demonstrate the most common techniques for light search and rescue; and
3. Demonstrate safe techniques for debris removal and survivor extrication during search and rescue operations.

Unit Overview

Search and rescue consist of three separate operations:

1. Size-up involves assessing the situation and determining a safe action plan (using the nine-step size-up model).
2. Search involves locating survivors and documenting their location.
3. Rescue involves the procedures and methods required to extricate the survivors.

Previous disasters have shown that the first response to trapped survivors immediately after almost every disaster is by spontaneous, untrained, and well-intentioned persons who rush to the site of a collapse in an attempt to free the survivors.

Often, these spontaneous rescue efforts result in serious injuries and compounded problems. Plan and practice rescue efforts in advance. People, including rescuers, have died when the rescuers were not prepared and trained.

Deciding to Attempt Rescue

The decision to attempt a rescue should be based on three factors:

1. Risks involved to both the rescuer and the survivor;
2. The overall goal of doing the greatest good for the greatest number of people; and
3. Resources and labor available.

Goals of Search and Rescue

The goals of search and rescue operations are to:

- Rescue the greatest number of people in the shortest amount of time;
- Get the walking wounded and ambulatory survivors out first;
- Rescue lightly trapped survivors next; and
- Keep the rescuers and survivors safe.

Effective Search and Rescue

Effective search and rescue operations hinge on:

- Effective size-up;
- Rescuer safety; and

- Survivor safety

This unit focuses on the components of an effective search and rescue operation—size-up, search, and rescue—and the methods and techniques that rescuers can use to locate and safely remove survivors.

SECTION 2: SAFETY DURING SEARCH AND RESCUE OPERATIONS

CERT Search and Rescue Size-up

Like all CERT operations, search and rescue requires size-up at the beginning of the operation and throughout its duration. As a reminder, size-up steps include:

- Gathering facts;
- Assessing damage;
- Considering probabilities;
- Assessing your situation;
- Establishing priorities;
- Making decisions;
- Developing a plan of action;
- Taking action; and
- Evaluating progress.

Table 7.1: CERT Search and Rescue Size-up Checklist

Step 1: Gather Facts		
Time		
Does the time of day or week affect search and rescue efforts? How?	Yes	No
Type of Construction		
What type(s) of structure(s) is (are) involved?		
What type(s) of construction is (are) involved?		
What type(s) of terrain is (are) involved?		
Occupancy		
Are the structures occupied? If yes, how many people are likely to be affected?	Yes	No
Are there special considerations (e.g. children, elderly, pets, people with access and functional needs)? If yes, what are the special considerations?	Yes	No
Weather		
Will weather conditions affect your safety? If yes, how will your safety be affected?	Yes	No
Will weather conditions affect the search and rescue situation? If yes, how will the search and rescue situation be affected?	Yes	No

Step 1: Gather Facts		
Hazards		
Are hazardous materials involved? If yes, at what location?	Yes	No
Are any other types of hazards involved? Is yes, what other hazards?	Yes	No
Step 2: Assess and Communicate the Damage		
For structural searches, take a lap around the building. Is the damage beyond the CERT's capability? If yes, what special requirements or specifications are required?	Yes	No
Have you communicated the facts and the initial damage assessment to the appropriate person(s)?	Yes	No
Step 3: Consider Possibilities		
Is the situation stable?	Yes	No
Is there a great risk or potential for more disaster activity that will affect personal safety? If yes, what are the known risks?	Yes	No
What else could go wrong?	Yes	No
Step 4: Assess Your Own Situation		
What available resources do you have to attempt the search and rescue?		
What equipment is available?		
Step 5: Establish Priorities		
Can CERT volunteers attempt a search and rescue *safely*? If no, do not attempt a search and rescue.	Yes	No
Are there any other more pressing needs now? If yes, list.	Yes	No
Step 6: Make Decisions		
Where will deployment of available resources do the most good while maintaining an adequate margin of safety?		
Step 7: Develop Plan of Action		
Determine how best to deploy personnel and other resources.		
Step 8: Take Action		
Put the plan into effect.		

Step 9: Evaluate Progress
Continually size up the situation to identify changes in the scope of the problem, safety risks, and resources availability.

Step 1: Gather Facts

The facts of the situation must guide your search and rescue efforts. When gathering facts, CERT volunteers need to consider:

- The time of the event and day of the week.
  - At night, more people will be in their homes, so the greatest need for search and rescue will be in residential settings. Conversely, during the day, people will be at work, so the need will be in commercial buildings. The locations of people in their homes and the amount of daylight available may also affect search and rescue operations.
- Construction type and terrain.
  - Some types of construction are more susceptible to damage and the type of terrain will affect how best to conduct the search.
- Occupancy.
  - The design purpose of the structure may indicate the likely number of survivors and their location.
- Weather.
  - Severe weather will impact survivors and rescuers alike and will hamper rescue efforts. Consider forecasts of severe weather as a limiting factor on the period during which search and rescue can occur.
- Hazards.
  - Knowledge of other potential hazards in the general and immediate areas is important to search and rescue efforts. For example, if you suspect a gas leak, taking the time to locate and shut off the gas can have a big impact in terms of loss of life.

Exercise 7.1: Gathering Facts

Purpose: This exercise will give you the opportunity to consider some of the facts that CERT search and rescue teams will need to gather during size-up.

Instructions:

- Refer to the Scenario handout.
- Brainstorm the following questions:
  - What does this scenario tell you about the probable density for the affected area?
  - What does this scenario tell you about the facts that volunteers must gather?
  - What impact could these facts have on search and rescue operations?
  - What kinds of search and rescue operations are probable?
  - What, if any, are the constraints that search and rescue personnel may face in this scenario?

— Can volunteers overcome constraints within the established CERT mission? If so, how?

Scenario

At 2:30 p.m. on Tuesday, August 9, a squall line passed through your town. Because of the difference in barometric pressure on either side of the front, a "gust front" with straight-line winds of more than 70 miles per hour preceded the squall line. Continued strong winds and extremely heavy rain followed the gust front. The town loses electricity.

You activate in accordance with your CERT program's standard operating procedures (SOPs). On the way to the staging area at the local high school, you notice considerable damage, including felled trees and utility lines. Many streets are impassable, making you take a roundabout route to the high school. As you make your way to the staging area, you see that the roof has blown off of a large portion of a local shopping center and that the exterior wall on the west end of the structure has collapsed.

After reaching the staging area, you check in with the Logistics Team Leader, who assigns you to Search and Rescue Team 2. Although CERT volunteers cannot venture into the section of the shopping center that has collapsed, Search and Rescue Team 2 will be searching near the collapsed area to see if there are survivors in that area.

Step 2: Assess and Communicate Damage

There are general guidelines for assessing damage in interior searches and exterior searches. When in doubt about the condition of a building, CERT volunteers should always use the more cautious assessment. If you are unsure about whether damage to a building is moderate or heavy, CERT volunteers should assume heavy damage. The CERT mission changes depending on the amount of structural damage.

CERT Mission and Types of Damages

The CERT mission for interior searches depends on if damage is light, moderate, or heavy.

Damage is Light

The CERT mission is to locate; assess; treat airway, major bleeding, and low body temperature; continue size-up; and document.

Light damage includes:

- Superficial damage;
- Broken windows;
- Superficial cracks or breaks in the wall surface, for example, fallen or cracked plaster; and
- Minor damage to the interior contents.

Damage is Moderate

The CERT mission is to locate; treat airway, major bleeding, and low body temperature; evacuate; warn others; continue size-up while minimizing the number of rescuers and time spent inside the structure.

Moderate damage includes:

- Visible signs of damage;
- Decorative work damaged or fallen;
- Many visible cracks or breaks in the wall surface;
- Major damage to interior contents; and
- Building still on foundation.

Damage is Heavy

The CERT mission is to secure the building perimeter and warn others of the danger in entering the building.

Heavy damage includes:

- Partial or total collapse;
- Tilting;
- Obvious structural instability;
- Building off foundation;
- Heavy smoke or fire;
- Gas leaks/hazardous materials inside; and
- Rising or moving water.

CERT volunteers are not to enter a building with heavy damage under any circumstances.

Assessing Damage

Assessing the damage of a building or structure will require an examination from all sides. Be sure to do an initial "lap around" the building.

In assessing damage, CERT personnel must consider probable levels of damage based on the type and age of construction.

In addition to a visual assessment, rescuers should also "listen" to damaged structures. If a building is creaking or "groaning," it is unstable and volunteers should not enter it.

Communicating Damage

You can describe different locations within and around the structure by using the ABCD standard, with A corresponding to the front of the building and B, C, and D representing the sides of the building moving clockwise from A.

Using this system, volunteers can break down the area inside of a structure by quadrants to facilitate communication. For instance, a hazard or survivor located closest to the A and B sides of the structure is in the A/B quadrant.

Remember, you must communicate your findings to the CERT command post or responding agencies.

Table 7.2: Probable Severity and Type of Earthquake Damage Based on Construction Type

Construction Type	Description	Probable Damage Areas	Severity
Single-Family Dwelling	• Wood frame	• Masonry chimney • Utilities	Light
	• Pre-1933	• Foundation movement • Utilities • Porches	Moderate
	• Hillside	• Unique hazards • Ground failure	Heavy
Multi-Family Dwelling	• Up-and-down and/or side-by side living units	• Soft first floor • Utilities	Moderate
Unreinforced Brick	• Pre-1933 construction • Lime or sand mortar • "King Row" or • "Soldier Row" (bricks turned on end every 5-7 rows) • Reinforcing plates • Arched windows and doors • Recessed windows and doors	• Walls collapse, then roof	Heavy
Tilt-up	• Large warehouses and plants • Concrete slabs lifted into place • Walls in set approximately 6-8 inches • Lightweight roof construction	• Roof collapses, then walls	Heavy
High-Rise	• Steel reinforced	• Broken glass • Content movement • Exterior trim and fascia	Light

Step 3: Consider Probabilities

Because you will be working in close proximity to the dangerous situation, considering what will probably happen and what could happen are of critical importance. Be sure to identify potentially life-threatening hazards and ask:

- How stable is the situation?
  - Even within a structure that appears from the outside to have only minimal or moderate damage, nonstructural damage or instability inside the structure can pose real danger to the rescue team. CERT volunteers should think about what they already know about the structure that has been damaged. Are lawn chemicals, paints, or other potentially hazardous materials stored within the structure? How are they stored? Where are

they? It will not take CERT volunteers much time to answer these types of questions, but the answers could make a huge difference in how they approach the search.

- What secondary factors should CERT volunteers consider?
    - Take a moment to look around and assess the situation outside of the immediate area. What is the weather doing? Is the wind changing? Is a storm moving in that would affect the response? Is there a crowd growing? Are there very few people around? Do you hear first responders in the distance, or is everything quiet?
- What else could go wrong?
    - Based on the information gathered during Steps 1 and 2 of the size-up, CERT volunteers should take a few moments to play "What if?" to try to identify additional risks that they may face. What happens if the power goes out during the search? What if a wall that appears stable shifts and collapses? Applying "Murphy's Law" to the situation could save CERT volunteers' lives.
- What does it all mean for the search and rescue?
    - Based on the probabilities, CERTs should think about what they can do to reduce the risks associated with the probabilities that they have identified. Is a spotter necessary to look for movement that could indicate a possible collapse and warn the rescue team? Is some remedial action required to stabilize nonstructural hazards before beginning the search? CERT search and rescue teams must remember that their own safety is the priority.

Step 4: Assess Your Situation

Remember that size-up is a compounding process, with each step building upon the previous steps until the decision is made to either begin the search and rescue operation or that the situation is not safe to begin. You need to draw on everything you learned from Steps 1 through 3 to assess your situation to determine:

- Whether the situation is safe enough to continue;
- The risks that rescuers will face if they continue; and
- The available resources volunteers will need to conduct the operation safely.

Assessing resources, including personnel, tools, and equipment, is extremely important to search and rescue operations.

Rescue Resources

Search and rescue resources include personnel, equipment, and tools. Below, find questions that you should ask yourself regarding the availability of these types of resources.

Table 7.3: Search and Rescue Resource Planning Questions

Resource	Planning Questions
Personnel	• How many trained CERT volunteers are available for this operation? • Who lives and/or works in the area? • During what hours are these people most likely to be available? • What skills or hobbies do they have that might be useful in search and rescue operations? • What might be the most effective means of mobilizing their efforts? • Do all team members have everyone else's cell number?
Equipment	• What equipment is available locally that might be useful for search and rescue? • Where is it located? • How can volunteers access it? • On which structures (or types of structures) might it be most effective?
Tools	• What tools are available that might be useful to lift, move, or cut disaster debris? • What tools are available that will aid communication?

Step 5: Establish Priorities

After evaluating the situation and keeping in mind that the safety of the CERT volunteer is always the top priority, the next step is to determine:

- What should be done; and
- In what order.

The safety of CERT volunteers is always the first priority and will dictate some of the other priorities. For example, volunteers must complete the task of removing or mitigating known hazards before teams begin to search. Think through the situation logically to determine how you should approach the operation.

Priority determinations are based on:

- The safety of CERT volunteers;
- Life safety for survivors and others;
- Protection of the environment; and
- Protection of property.

Remember your goal: Rescue the greatest number in the shortest amount of time, but not at the expense of your own safety.

Step 6: Make Decisions

At this point in the size-up you will make decisions about where to deploy your resources to do the most good while maintaining an adequate margin of safety. You will base many of your decisions on the priorities established during Step 5.

Step 7: Develop Plan of Action

Step 7 is where all of the information you have about the situation comes together. During Step 7, the CERT Team Leader (TL) will decide specifically how the team will conduct its operation, considering the highest priority tasks first.

You do not have to write down an action plan, but when search and rescue operations are required, the situation is probably complex enough that a written plan of some type will be important.

A plan should:

- Help focus the operation on established priorities and decisions.
- Provide for documentation to give to responding agencies when they arrive on scene.
- Provide for documentation that will become part of the record of the CERT's overall operation.

Keep notes as you develop your action plan. Volunteers should document any changes made to the initial plan based on new information that emerges.

Step 8: Take Action

This step involves putting the plan developed in Step 7 into action.

Step 9: Evaluate Progress

Step 9, Evaluate Progress, is the most critical step, not only in terms of evaluating whether the plan works, but also from a safety standpoint.

Remember that size-up is ongoing and that information gained during Step 9 needs to be fed back into the decision-making process for possible revision of priorities and updated action planning.

Specific Safety Considerations

Regardless of the severity of structural damage, rescuer safety must be the primary concern. The most frequent causes of rescuer deaths are disorientation and secondary collapse.

Follow these guidelines during all search and rescue operations:

- Use a buddy system.
  - Successful search and rescue depend on teamwork.
- Be alert for hazards (e.g., power lines, natural gas leaks, hazardous materials, sharp objects).
  - You should never attempt to search an area where water is rising.
- Use safety equipment.
  - Wearing gloves and a helmet will protect a rescuer's hands and head. Kneepads, coveralls, and thick-soled boots will protect a rescuer from glass and other sharp objects found on the ground following many natural disasters. The primary cause of rescuer problems after working in a

structural collapse is breathing dust, so a dust mask is essential. However, a dust mask will not filter out all harmful materials. If volunteers suspect the presence of chemical or biological agents, they must evacuate to an upwind location and notify professional responders.

- Have backup teams available to allow rotation of teams, prevent fatigue, and ensure help if a team gets into trouble. Have teams drink fluids and eat to keep themselves fresh.

Exercise 7.2: Search and Rescue Size-up

Purpose: This exercise is an interactive activity that will provide an opportunity to practice some of the thinking processes involved in planning and search and rescue size-up.

The brainstorming required will help you to begin to assess your neighborhoods or workplaces in terms of building structures, hazardous materials, and any necessary safety precautions.

Instructions:

1. Assemble in groups of four or five.
2. Read the scenario given to you by the instructor.
3. Designate a recorder and, given the disaster and the specific building, answer the following questions:
   - What are the pertinent facts that must be gathered?
     What kind of prediction can you make regarding damage, based on the incident and the building construction?
   - What probable search and rescue problems can you identify?
   - What specific safety considerations can you identify?
4. Select a spokesperson to present the group's responses to the class.

SECTION 3: CONDUCTING INTERIOR AND EXTERIOR SEARCH OPERATIONS

When a CERT makes the decision to initiate search operations, CERT volunteers will inspect the area assigned by the CERT TL. The search operation involves two processes:

- Employing search techniques based on the size-up; and
- Locating survivors.

By using these processes, search operations will be more efficient, thorough, and safe. They will also facilitate later rescue operations. Although the processes are related, this section addresses them one at a time. Interior search operations are the most common and discussed first; exterior search operations will be discussed later in this unit.

Locating Potential Survivors in a Structure

The first step in locating potential survivors in a structure is to gather more precise information about damage and to develop priorities and plans by conducting a size-up of the interior of the building. The data gathered will provide more information about possible areas of entrapment or voids.

Structural Voids

There are several types of structural voids:

- Pancake void
- Lean-to void
- "V" void

Survivors may be trapped in a structural void. If you hear any signs of life coming from a structural void, report it to the TL immediately and make appropriate markings to direct professional rescuers, but do not attempt the rescue yourself. Attempting to rescue a person from a structural void without proper equipment may result in completing the collapse and harming the trapped person.

If CERT volunteers see collapsed floors or walls, they should leave the premises immediately.

Individual Voids

Individual voids are spaces into which the survivor may have crawled for protection. Examples of individual voids include bathtubs and the space underneath desks. Children may seek shelter in smaller places like cabinets.

After identifying the possible areas of entrapment, CERT volunteers must:

- Determine the potential number of survivors; and
- Identify the most probable areas of entrapment.

Some information may be known through assessment, but CERT volunteers may need to get some information by talking to bystanders or those who are familiar with the structure.

CERT volunteers should ask questions when talking with these individuals, including:

- How many people live (or work) in the building?
- Where would they be at this time?
- What is the building layout?
- What have you seen or heard?
- Has anyone come out?
- What are the normal exit routes from the building?

Be aware that the event may confuse bystanders. They may tend to exaggerate potential numbers or may not even remember the event accurately. Gather as much information as you can, though, because it will be useful for planning search priorities and implementing the search.

Search Methodology

An effective search methodology:

- Indicates rescuer location;
- Locates survivors as quickly and safely as possible; and
- Prevents duplication of effort.

Search Markings

Experienced search and rescue personnel use the following system. CERTs will use the same system. This will save time for fellow CERT volunteers and other responders during the search and continual size-up of the structure.

Upon entering a search area, you will make a mark next to the door to indicate that you are entering. Do not make the mark on the door or on the wall where the door swings. Make a single slash and write the agency or group ID at the "9 o'clock" position. Then write the date and "time in" at the "12 o'clock" position.

Upon exiting the search area, make another slash to form an "X" (the agency or group ID will be in the left quadrant). Enter the search "time out" In the top quadrant.

- **Right quadrant:** Enter the areas of the structure searched and any specific information about hazards.
- **Lower quadrant:** Enter information about the survivors found in the search area. "L" represents living and "D" represents dead. The search marking on the front of a structure or building should contain the total number of survivors, whereas search markings inside the structure or building will include survivor totals for specific search areas. Indicate where survivors were taken.

Search Methodology

- Use the buddy system.
  - Always remain within arm's reach of at least one other CERT volunteer when conducting an interior search. This is to enable assistance in the event of a slip or a fall and to be able to push or pull one another out of harm's way.

- Upon entering each space or room, call out to survivors.
  - Shout something like, "If anyone can hear my voice, come here." If any survivors come to you, ask them for any information that they may have about the building or others who may be trapped then, depending on the condition of the building, give them further directions such as, "Stay here" or "Wait outside".

Remember that even those who are able to get to you may be in shock and confused. When giving directions to survivors, CERT volunteers should look directly at the survivors, speak in short sentences, and keep their directions simple.

Use a systematic search pattern. Ensure that all areas of the building are covered. Examples of systematic search patterns to use include:

- Bottom-up/top-down; and
- Right wall/left wall.

Keep in mind that every interior space has six sides — including the floor and ceiling. Rescuers must check all six sides to locate hazards such as fixtures that may be hanging from the ceiling

- **Stop frequently to listen:** Listen for tapping, movement, or voices.
- **Triangulate:** Consider using triangulation when a potential survivor's location is obscured. If access permits, three rescuers, guided by survivor sounds, form a triangle around the area and direct flashlights into the area. The light shining from different directions will eliminate shadows that could otherwise hide survivors. Triangulation should not be used as an initial search method.
- **Report results:** Keep complete records both of removed survivors and of survivors who remain trapped or are dead. Report this information to emergency services personnel when they reach the scene.

Exterior Search

In addition to searching inside a structure, CERT volunteers may need to search open areas outside of buildings.

Conducting an effective search in open areas requires that searchers work methodically and follow standard procedures established by those in charge of the search operation. This is true in all cases, especially if the area is a crime scene, where all potential evidence must be protected.

If searchers are needed, they should assemble in a central staging area and sign in. Authorities will brief the searchers on what they will be looking for, what areas they are responsible for searching, the pattern of the search, and what they should do if they discover the missing person, evidence, or related information.

Exterior search patterns include grid, line, quadrant or zone, and spiral. Typically, a grid pattern is used in large open areas or small areas when a hands-and-knees search is conducted.

Grid is one of the most commonly used types of search patterns. Keep the guidelines below in mind when conducting a grid search.

- View the search area as a grid, with searchers initially positioned at one side of the grid.
- The distance between the searchers should be set according to visibility and debris. In all cases, searchers must remain within line of sight and voice contact with searchers on either side of them.
- It is critical that the area assigned to each searcher overlaps that of the searchers on either side of them.
- The searchers proceed, maintaining as straight a line as possible across the entire search area. As each searcher moves across the area, they conduct a thorough search for survivors within their designated row of the grid.
- To ensure full coverage, CERTs must record each area searched.
- A grid search might be particularly useful following a tornado or hurricane.

SECTION 4: CONDUCTING RESCUE OPERATIONS

Rescues involve three primary functions:

1. Moving objects and debris to create a safe rescue environment and free survivors;
2. Assessing survivors, checking for life-threatening conditions such as airway obstruction, severe bleeding, and low body temperature; and
3. Removing survivors as safely and as quickly as possible.

Creating a Safe Environment

There are three safety considerations for all rescue operations:

1. Maintain rescuer safety;
2. Assess survivors in lightly and moderately damaged buildings; and
3. Evacuate survivors as quickly as possible from moderately damaged buildings while minimizing additional injury.

CERTs cannot achieve these considerations without creating as safe an environment as possible before attempting rescue. Therefore, there are certain precautions that rescuers must take to minimize risk.

Precautions to Minimize Risk

There are certain precautions that rescuers must take to minimize risk and increase their chances of achieving their rescue goals.

- **Know Your Limitations:** Many volunteers have been injured or killed during rescue operations because they did not pay attention to their own physical and mental limitations. CERT rescuers should take the time to drink fluids, eat, relax, and rest so that they can return with a clear mind and improved energy.
- **Follow Safety Procedures:** CERT volunteers should always use the proper safety equipment required for the situation and follow established procedures, including:
  — Work in pairs.
  — Assess and treat only in lightly damaged buildings.
  — In moderately damaged buildings, assess only and remove survivors as quickly as possible.
  — Never enter an unstable structure.
  — Lift by bending the knees, keeping the back straight, and pushing up with the legs.
  — Carry the load close to the body.
  — Lift and carry no more than is reasonable.
- **Remove Debris:** Remove debris as needed to minimize risk to rescuers and to free entrapped survivors.

Image 7.1: Proper Body Position for Lifting

Proper body position for lifting showing the back straight and lifting with the knees.

Leveraging and Cribbing

You may encounter situations in which moving debris is needed to free survivors. In these situations, CERT rescuers should consider leveraging and cribbing to move and stabilize the debris until the rescue is complete.

- Leveraging is accomplished by wedging a lever under the object that needs to be moved, with a stationary object underneath it to act as a fulcrum. When the lever is forced down over the fulcrum, the far end of the lever will lift the object.
- A crib is a wooden framework used for support or strengthening the object.
    - Box cribbing means arranging pairs of wood pieces alternately to form a stable rectangle.
    - You may use a variety of cribbing materials for these procedures and you will need to improvise by using materials such as tires or structural debris. Whatever you use, do not put form over function.

Volunteers may use leveraging and cribbing together by alternately lifting the object and placing cribbing materials underneath the lifted edge to stabilize it.

Safety is number one: "Lift an inch; crib an inch." Leveraging and cribbing should be gradual for stability, safety, and efficiency.

It may also be necessary to use leveraging and cribbing at more than one location (e.g., front and back) to ensure stability. Never leverage and crib on opposite ends at the same time because doing so will increase the instability of the debris. If leveraging is required at both ends, lift and crib at one end, then repeat the process at the other end.

Positioning the lever and the fulcrum correctly is critical for safe operations. The fulcrum and pry tool must be perpendicular (90 degrees) to the edge of the object being lifted. Attempting to leverage a heavy object using too sharp an angle is inefficient and can result in back injury.

Box cribbing is stable, but it requires pieces of cribbing material of relatively uniform size. When such material is not available, "unboxed" cribbing can also work effectively to support and stabilize the heavy object.

When you are able to achieve sufficient lift, you should remove the survivor and reverse the leveraging and cribbing procedure to lower the object. You should never leave an unsafe condition unless the event has left the structure or building obviously compromised.

When you must remove debris to locate survivors, you should set up a human chain and pass the debris from one person to the next. Be careful, however, to set up the chain in a position that will not interfere with rescue operations.

Wear your PPE to protect yourself always. Kneepads can be an important addition to your PPE during rescue operations.

Leveraging and Cribbing Steps

Step 1: Conduct a size-up of the scene. Gather facts, identify hazards, and establish priorities.

Step 2: Have one person in charge and formulate a plan of action, based upon the information you have received, to identify how and where to lift and crib and to determine how you will remove the survivor from underneath the debris.

Step 3: Gather necessary materials for lifting/cribbing operations: lever, fulcrum, cribbing blocks, spacers/wedges. During an actual emergency, you may have to use creative, substitute materials.

Step 4: Use cribbing materials to stabilize the object prior to lifting.

Step 5: Distribute cribbing materials as necessary to be readily accessible during the lifting operation.

Step 6: Prepare to lift the object: Assemble the lever and fulcrum at the previously identified location.

Step 7: Assign a person to monitor and be ready to remove the survivor as soon as possible.

Step 8: Initiate the lift, using the lever and fulcrum for mechanical advantage.

Step 9: As the object is lifted, add cribbing as needed, one layer at a time.

Step 10: Once the object is adequately supported, remove the lever and fulcrum. You may then remove the survivor.

Step 11: Unless the event has left the structure obviously compromised, requiring you to evacuate immediately, reinitiate the lift and begin removing cribbing materials, reversing the process by which you built the crib.

Step 12: Progressively lower the object to the ground. Always return the heavy object to a stable position unless you have to evacuate immediately.

Step 13: Before you leave, remember to collect the lifting/cribbing supplies to be available for additional operations.

Image 7.2: Leveraging and Cribbing

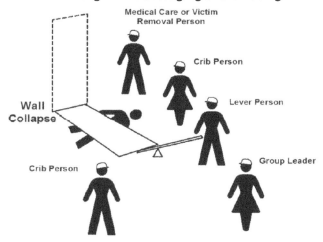

Team Organization for Leveraging/Cribbing Operations

Team organization for leveraging/cribbing operation, showing the survivor underneath a collapsed wall and the CERT volunteers at the following locations:

- **Group Leader:** In front of collapse, positioned so that he or she can view the entire operation while remaining out of the rescuers' way;
- **Lever Person:** At the front edge of the collapsed wall and positioned so that he or she can position a fulcrum and lever under the wall;
- **Crib Persons:** On either side of the collapsed wall and positioned to enable the placement of cribbing as the wall is raised with the lever; and
- **Medical Care/Survivor Removal Person:** Next to the Crib Person who is closest to the survivor's head.

Image 7.3: Box Cribbing

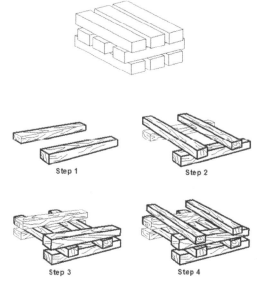

Four Steps to Box Building

Steps for building box cribbing:

Step 1: Position two pieces of wood parallel to each other on either side of the collapse.

Step 2: Place two pieces of wood perpendicularly across the base pieces.

Steps 3 and 4: Add additional layers of wood, with each perpendicular to the previous level.

Removing Survivors

The basic types of survivor removal are:

- Self-removal or assist; and
- Lifts and drags.

It is usually best to allow an ambulatory survivor to extricate him or herself. Be aware that ambulatory survivors are not always as strong and free of injury as they believe. When survivors are freed, they may need assistance to exit the structure.

Extrication Method

The type of extrication method selected should depend on the:

- General stability of the immediate environment;
- Number of rescuers available;
- Strength and ability of the rescuers; and
- Condition of the survivor.

If safety and time permit, you should not use lifts and drags to remove survivors when you suspect the survivors have closed-head or spinal injuries. In such cases, stabilize the spine using a backboard. You can use doors, tables, and similar materials as improvised backboards. The backboard must be able to carry the person and remember to use proper lifting techniques.

When moving survivors, rescuers must use teamwork and communication and try to keep the survivor's spine in a straight line. Remember, rescuer safety and the condition of the building will dictate the approach.

One-Person Arm Carry

If a rescuer is physically able and the survivor is small, the rescuer may use the one-person arm carry to lift and carry the survivor by:

- Reaching around the survivor's back and under the knees; and
- Lifting the survivor while keeping your back straight and lifting with your legs. Consider the size of the survivor and the distance in which you will need to carry him or her before using this carry.

Image 7.4: One-Person Arm Carry

One-Person Arm Carry with rescuer holding survivor around the back and under the knees.

Pack-Strap Carry

Another way for a single rescuer to lift a survivor safely is by using the one-person pack-strap carry. Using this method, you should:

Step 1: Stand with your back to the survivor.

Step 2: Place the survivor's arms over your shoulders and grab the hands in front of your chest.

Step 3: Hoist the survivor by bending forward slightly, until the survivor's feet just clear the floor.

*Note: The pack-strap carry is most effective for quick removal of a survivor over a short distance.

Image 7.5: Pack-Strap Carry

One-Person Pack-Strap Carry in which the rescuer places the survivor's arms over his or her shoulders and grabs the survivor's wrists over his or her chest, then hoists the survivor by bending over slightly.

Two-Person Carry

Survivor removal is easier when multiple rescuers are available. The survivor's upper body will weigh more than his or her lower body; therefore, position rescuers with greater body strength at the survivor's upper body. Two rescuers working together can remove a survivor using a two-person carry.

Rescuer 1: Squat at the survivor's head and grasp the survivor from behind around the midsection. Reach under the arms and grasp the survivor's left wrist with rescuer's right hand, and vice versa. Crossing the wrists creates a more secure hold on the survivor, pulling their arms and elbows closer to their body. This will be helpful if rescuers need to carry the survivor through any narrow passages.

Rescuer 2: Squat between the survivor's knees, facing either toward or away from the survivor. Note that, if the rescuers will carry the survivor over uneven areas such as stairs, the rescuers will need to face each other. Grasp the outside of the survivor's legs at the knees.

Both rescuers: Rise to a standing position simultaneously, keeping backs straight and lifting with the legs. Walk the survivor to safety.

Image 7.6: Two-Person Carry

Two-person Carry in which Rescuer 1 squats at the survivor's head and grasps the survivor from behind at the midsection. Rescuer 1 should use his right hand to grab the survivor's right wrist, and vice versa. Rescuer 2 squats between the survivor's knees, grasping the outside of the knees. Both rescuers rise to the standing position. *

Chair Carry

Two rescuers can also remove a survivor by seating him or her on a chair:

Rescuer 1: Cross the survivor's arms in his or her lap. Facing the back of the chair, grasp the back upright.

Rescuer 2: Grasp the two front legs of the chair.

Both rescuers: Tilt the chair back, lift simultaneously, and walk out.

It is best to use a sturdy, non-swivel chair for this lift.

*Note: If rescuers will need to carry the survivor over uneven surfaces, such as stairs, the rescuers must face each other.

Image 7.7: Chair Carry

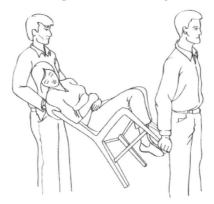

Chair Carry in which the survivor is placed in a sturdy, non-swivel chair and tilted backwards as rescuers lift the survivor. This lift requires two rescuers. If possible, secure the survivor to the chair. *

Blanket Carry

Use the blanket carry for survivors you cannot remove by other means. The blanket carry requires four to six rescuers to ensure stability for the survivor and one rescuer designated the lead person:

Step 1: Position a blanket next to the survivor, ensuring that the blanket will extend under the survivor's head.

Step 2: Tuck the blanket under the survivor and assist the survivor in moving to the center of the blanket. If necessary, use the log rolling technique to position them on the blanket.

Step 3: With three rescuers squatting on each side, roll up the edges of the blanket against the survivor to grasp a "handle." The lead person checks the team for even weight distribution and correct lifting position.

Step 4: The lead person calls out, "Ready to lift on the count of three: One, two, three, lift."

Step 5: The team lifts and stands in unison—keeping the survivor level—and carries the survivor feet first.

***Note:** that if rescuers will need to carry the survivor over uneven surfaces, such as stairs, the rescuers must face each other.

The team must also lower the survivor together, using the following steps:

Step 1: The lead person calls out, "Ready to lower on the count of three: One, two, three, lower."

Step 2: The team lowers the survivor in unison, exercising caution to keep the survivor level.

You can use a variety of materials — such as blankets, carpets, and folded tables — as improvised stretchers.

Log Rolling

Rescuers should use the "log rolling" technique to move survivors with a suspected or confirmed cervical spine injury. If the survivor is unconscious, assume he or she has a cervical spine injury. The rescuer at a survivor's head should give commands as fellow rescuers roll the survivor as a single unit onto the blanket, backboard, or other support.

Drag/Blanket Drag

When a rescuer is not able to carry a survivor, they can drag the survivor by grasping either the feet or the shoulders and dragging him or her clear of the hazard. If a blanket is available, use the blanket drag by following these steps:

Step 1: Wrap the survivor in a blanket.

Step 2: Squat down and grasp an edge of the blanket. Step 3: Drag the survivor across the floor.

Image 7.8: Correct Drag Technique

Correct drag technique, showing the rescuer grasping the survivor by either the feet or shoulders and dragging him or her clear of the hazard.

Image 7.9 - Blanket Drag

Blanket drag, showing the survivor wrapped in a blanket with the rescuer squatting at the survivor's head. The rescuer grasps the blanket behind the survivor's head and drags him or her clear of the hazard.

Exercise 7.3: Survivor Carries

Purpose: This exercise will provide you with an opportunity to practice different drags and carries designed for safe movement of survivors.

Instructions:

1. Break into teams of seven.
2. Members of your team will volunteer to be "survivors" that other team members will move using the drags and carries demonstrated in the class.
3. Use chairs and other items as needed to perform the drags and carries.
4. Be sure to trade off "survivor" and "rescuer" roles so that everyone on your team has a chance to practice the drags and carries.
5. Remember to know your limits! Do not attempt any lift or carry that will not be safe for you and the survivor.

Exercise 7.4: Survivor Extrication

Purpose: This exercise will provide you with an opportunity to practice the removal of entrapped survivors from a damage site, using leveraging/cribbing and drags and carries.

Instructions:

1. Break into teams of seven.
2. Your team will be directed to a "collapse site." Consider your plan of action.
3. Enter the "collapse site" and conduct a room search. Locate survivors and make a plan for extricating them from the debris.
4. Use leveraging and cribbing procedures as needed to free the survivor.
5. Use appropriate lifts and drags to remove survivors from the room (and, if possible, from the building).
6. If there is a second "collapse site," conduct another rescue operation.

UNIT 7 SUMMARY

The key points from this unit are:

- Base the decision to attempt a rescue on:
  - The risks involved; and
  - Achievement of the overall goal of doing the greatest good for the greatest number.
- The objectives of interior and exterior search and rescue are to:
  - Maintain rescuer safety at all times;
  - Rescue the greatest number of people in the shortest amount of time;
  - Get the walking wounded and ambulatory survivors out first; and
  - Rescue the lightly trapped survivors next.
- Remember that CERTs are restricted to light search and rescue. Your mission when dealing with heavily damaged structures or situations that are clearly unsafe (e.g., rising or swiftly moving water) is to warn others.
- Search and rescue size-up follows the same process as other CERT size-up operations. Size-up continues throughout search and rescue efforts and provides information about how to proceed. Remember: the CERT mission is to ensure safety and organization during the evaluation. Therefore, if the size-up indicates that evacuation of the team is necessary, do so immediately.
- When the decision to begin search operations is made, CERT searchers must:
  - Remember that the first priority is volunteer safety;
  - Employ appropriate search techniques; and
  - Locate any survivors and check for life threatening injuries.
- Locating survivors means completing a size-up of the building interior to identify areas of entrapment, then conducting a search that:
  - Is systematic and thorough;
  - Avoids unnecessary duplication of effort; and
  - Documents results.
- Rescue involves these main functions:
  - Moving objects and debris to create a safe rescue environment and free survivors;
  - Assessing or stabilizing survivors by checking for life-threatening conditions (airway obstruction, severe bleeding, and low body temperature); and
  - Removing survivors as safely and as quickly as possible based on the size-up.
- Remember that rescuer safety is always the top priority.
- Rescue operations hinge on maintaining rescuer safety, which requires CERT volunteers to recognize their own limitations. CERT volunteers should never attempt anything that exceeds their limitations at that point in time.
- Rescuers may leverage and crib to lift heavy debris and give access to trapped survivors.
- Rescuers can remove survivors in several ways, depending on:
  - Their condition;

- — The number of rescuers available;
- — The strength and ability of the rescuers; and
- — The stability of the environment.
- Stabilize survivors with suspected head or spinal injuries on some type of backboard before removing. When possible, defer these removals to trained EMS personnel.

Homework Assignment

Read and become familiar with the unit covered in the next session.

CERT Unit 8:
Terrorism and CERT

Participant Manual

CERT Unit 8: Terrorism and CERT

In this unit, you will learn about:

- **Terrorism:** Defining terrorism, including the goals and tactics of some terrorist groups, and detailing how to respond when an active shooter is in your vicinity.

- **Eight Signs of Terrorism:** The eight signs of terrorism and how to report suspicious activity.

- **Preparing for Your Neighborhood:** Steps to take to be prepared at home, work, and in your neighborhood.

- **Hazmat and CBRNE:** Identifying some basic guidelines during a Hazmat or CBRNE event.

CERT Unit 8 Table of Contents

SECTION 1: UNIT 8 OVERVIEW

Unit Objectives

At the end of this unit, you should be able to:

1. Define terrorism;
2. List the eight signs of terrorism and describe how to report suspicious activity;
3. Explain the role of a CERT volunteer during a terrorist incident; and
4. Describe activities to prepare for a terrorist incident at home, at work, and in the community.

SECTION 2: TERRORIST GOALS AND TACTICS

The U.S. Department of Justice's definition of terrorism:

> *"The unlawful use of force or violence against persons or property to intimidate or coerce a government, the civilian population, or any segment thereof, in furtherance of political or social objectives."*

Terrorism may be perpetrated by foreign or domestic individuals or groups and although the results are similar, these groups may select different targets and use different tactics to achieve their goals.

Terrorist Goals

Terrorists use violence to influence government policy and to achieve specific objectives for their cause. Attacks are intended to undermine the public's sense of safety and their confidence in the government. Attackers seek to portray the government as ineffective, weak, and/or otherwise incapable.

Terrorist attacks are often perpetrated by ideological extremists who are prepared to die in what they consider a symbolic sacrifice or act of martyrdom. Attackers frequently exploit social media seeking to spread misinformation and broadcast their actions to audiences around the globe, with the desire of increasing fear while simultaneously bolstering their credibility and legitimacy with like-minded supporters.

New Tactics

Recently, terrorist attacks have trended away from large resource intensive plots such as the September 11 attacks to more decentralized, less sophisticated attacks like those in Paris, France in 2016. Attackers have favored smaller, less centrally controlled networks, using more simplistic and accessible means such as guns and homemade improvised explosive devices (IEDs). These components are easier to acquire, control, and conceal than large high-yield explosives, biological, radiological, or nuclear devices. Although there is always some risk from CBRNE type incidents and the United States remains vigilant against these threats, it is difficult to obtain and deploy these types of weapons.

Active Shooter

An Active Shooter is an individual actively engaged in killing or attempting to kill people in a confined and populated area. In most cases, active shooters use firearms(s) and there is no pattern or method to their selection of targets. Active shooter situations are unpredictable and evolve quickly. Typically, the immediate deployment of law enforcement is required to stop the shooting and mitigate harm to survivors.

Many recent terrorist attacks have included armed individuals with some training indiscriminately shooting civilians; although the motivations are different than a single active shooter, the results are similar: rapidly accumulating casualties in a contained space.

Improvised Explosive Devices

An IED attack is the use of a "homemade" bomb and/or destructive device to destroy, incapacitate, harass, or distract. Because they are improvised, IEDs can come in many forms, ranging from a small pipe bomb to a sophisticated device capable of causing massive damage and loss of life.

Terrorist networks both domestic and abroad have published numerous sets of instructions on how to make homemade explosives. IEDs consist of a variety of components that include an initiator, switch, main charge, power source, and a container. IEDs can be worn (belts, vests), carried (bags, backpacks, containers of all sizes/types), or transported in a vehicle; placed or thrown by a person; delivered in a package; or concealed on the roadside.

To gain a better understanding of the impact that IEDs can have, the table below illustrates the damage radius cause by various sizes and types of IEDs.

Image 8.1: IED Impact

Threat	Threat Description	Explosive Capacity	Building Evacuation Distance	Outdoor Evacuation Distance
	Small Package/letter	1 lb	40 ft	900 ft
	Pipe Bomb	5 lb	70 ft	1,200 ft
	FedEx Package	10 lb	90 ft	1,080 ft
	Vest/Container Bombs	20 lb	110 ft	1,700 ft
	Parcel Package	50 lb	150 ft	1,850 ft
	Compact Car	500 lb	320 ft	1,900 ft
	Full Size Car/Minivan	1,000 lb	400 ft	2,400 ft
	Van/SUV/Pickup Truck	4,000 lb	640 ft	3,800 ft
	Delivery Truck	10,000 lb	860 ft	5,100 ft

IEDs may be surrounded by or packed with additional materials or "enhancements" such as nails, glass, or metal fragments designed to increase the amount of shrapnel propelled by the explosion to maximize casualties. Enhancements may also include other elements such as hazardous materials. An IED can be initiated by a variety of methods depending on the intended target.

Complex Coordinated Terrorist Attacks

A complex coordinated terrorist attack is a synchronized attack, conducted by two or more semi-independent teams at multiple locations in close succession, initiated with little or no warning, using well trained attackers and employing one or more of the following: fire arms, explosives, and fire as a weapon.

As seen in Paris, France in 2016, attackers have coordinated their actions to hit multiple targets nearly simultaneously. When conducting these attacks, there may be pre-planned coordination as well as real-time coordination between attackers. These attacks can be extremely lethal in a relatively short period of time.

Cyber Attacks

Another type of terrorist weapon is deliberate, large-scale disruption of computer networks. This is known as cyberterrorism. To help guard against cyberterrorism, it is important that computer users implement appropriate security measures.

Cybersecurity involves protecting infrastructure by preventing, detecting, and responding to cyber incidents. Unlike physical threats that prompt immediate action—like stop, drop, and roll in the event of a fire—cyber threats are often difficult to identify and comprehend. Among these dangers are viruses erasing entire systems, intruders breaking into systems and altering files, intruders using your computer or device to attack others, or intruders stealing confidential information. The spectrum of cyber risks is limitless. Threats, some more serious and sophisticated than others, can have wide-ranging effects at the individual, community, organizational, and national levels.

- Organized cybercrime, state-sponsored hackers, and cyber espionage can pose national security risks to our country.
- Transportation, power, and other services may be disrupted by large-scale cyber incidents. The extent of the disruption will be determined by many factors such as the target and size of the incident.
- Vulnerability to data breach and loss increases if an organization's network is compromised. Information about a company, its employees, and its customers can be at risk.
- Individually-owned devices such as computers, tablets, mobile phones, and gaming systems that connect to the Internet are vulnerable to intrusion. Personal information may be at risk without proper security.

SECTION 3: PREPARING YOUR COMMUNITY

If You See Something, Say Something: Potential Indicators

We all have a responsibility to play an active role in keeping the country safe. The phrase, "If you see something, say something," took on additional power after the foiled Times Square bomb plot in New York City. On May 1, 2010, street vendors in Times Square noticed a smoking SUV with its blinkers on, engine running, and no one inside. They decided to say something to a police officer. Thousands of people cleared from the area while the bomb was dismantled.

Eight Signs of Terrorism

The presence of even a few signs may indicate the possibility of a terrorist attack. It is important to understand what these signs may look like as they are executed so you are able to identify them within your community. If you recognize one of these signs being acted out, it is important to contact your local law enforcement and effectively communicate the suspicious activity that you have identified. The FBI's Suspicious Activity Reporting (SAR) tip line (https://tips.fbi.gov/) is an avenue for reporting any suspicious activities.

Signs exhibited by potential terrorists (often in this order) include:

- **Surveillance:** The targeted area is being watched and studied carefully. This may include recording or monitoring activities.
- **Elicitation:** Information is gathered that is specific to the intended target. This may be by mail, phone, or in person.
- **Tests of Security:** Local security measures are tested and analyzed, including measuring reaction times to security breaches or attempts to penetrate security.
- **Funding:** Raising, transferring, and spending money, which may include selling drugs or stolen merchandise, human trafficking, and funneling money through businesses or charities.
- **Acquiring Supplies:** Necessary supplies are gathered to prepare the attack, including weapons/weapon components, transportation, and communications. Supplies may be purchased with cash only.
- **Impersonation or Suspicious People Who Do Not Belong:** People impersonating roles to gain access or information and people who don't fit in or don't seem to belong in the location.
- **Rehearsal and Dry Runs:** Groups or individuals will often map out routes, determine traffic flow and timing ahead of time, and can also operate test runs before the actual attack.
- **Deployment:** The final and most urgent phase when terrorists are deploying assets and getting into position. Attack is imminent.

Although it is not the mission of CERT volunteers to keep constant watch for these signs, everyone should be alert to changes in their environment as a clue to a possible terrorist attack and report suspicious activities to appropriate authorities.

Potential Targets in Your Community

While hardened targets, such as government buildings, military installations, and infrastructure (e.g., power grids and dams) remain viable targets for certain groups, attacks have trended towards easier, less secure targets. Terrorists have frequently selected soft targets like schools, parks, large gathering spaces, cafés, and concert halls. Although differently motivated, active shooters in the United States have also selected less secure targets like malls, movie theatres, and universities. Smaller, less involved plots still generate high casualties and allow the attackers to achieve their objectives with fewer resources.

Preparedness

Terrorist attacks frequently occur without warning; however, being alert, reporting suspicious activities, and taking general preparedness steps, such as having a plan to communicate with loved ones, will help you if one does occur. If you believe a terrorist attack is imminent, call 9-1-1 and follow the instructions provided.

Exercise 8.1: Preparing for a Terrorism-Related Event

Purpose: As with all types of disasters and emergencies, preparation is key to planning for a terrorism-related event. Although it is often difficult to predict when such an event may occur, there are several steps that you can take today to be prepared.

Instructions:

1. Break into small table groups.
2. As a group, create a list of activities that CERT volunteers can do at home or work to better prepare for a terrorism related emergency. Be prepared to share your list with the rest of the class.

SECTION 4: ACTIVE SHOOTER SITUATIONS

As introduced in Section 1, active shooter situations are unpredictable and evolve quickly.

How to Respond When an Active Shooter is in Your Vicinity

Quickly determine the most reasonable way to protect your own life. Remember that customers and clients are likely to follow the lead of employees and managers during an active shooter situation.

1. RUN

If there is an accessible escape path, attempt to evacuate the premises. Be sure to:

- Have an escape route and plan in mind ahead of time;
- Evacuate regardless of whether others agree to follow;
- Leave your belongings behind;
- Help others escape, if possible;
- Prevent individuals from entering an area where the active shooter may be, if possible;
- Keep your hands visible;
- Follow the instructions of any police officers; and
- Call 9-1-1 when you are safe.

2. HIDE

If evacuation is not possible, find a place to hide where the active shooter is less likely to find you. Your hiding place should:

- Be out of the active shooter's view;
- Provide protection if shots are fired in your direction (i.e., an office with a closed and locked door); and
- Not trap you or restrict your options for movement.

To prevent an active shooter from entering your hiding place:

- Lock the door; and
- Blockade the door with heavy furniture.

If the active shooter is nearby:

- Lock the door;
- Silence your cell phone and/or pager;
- Turn off any source of noise (e.g., radios, televisions);
- Hide behind large items (e.g., cabinets, desks); and
- Remain quiet.

If evacuation and hiding out are not possible:

- Remain calm;
- Dial 9 -1-1, if possible, to alert police to the active shooter's location; and
- If you cannot speak, leave the line open and allow the dispatcher to listen.

3. FIGHT

If you are unable to run, evacuate or hide and when your life is in imminent danger, you may attempt to disrupt and/or incapacitate the active shooter by:

- Taking decisive action;
- Acting as aggressively as possible against him/her;
- Throwing items and improvising weapons;
- Yelling; and
- Committing to your actions.

How to Respond When Law Enforcement Arrives

Law enforcement's purpose is to stop the active shooter as soon as possible. Officers will proceed directly to the shooting without stopping to render aid to the survivors.

- Officers may arrive in teams;
- Officers may wear street clothes, regular patrol uniforms, or external bulletproof vests, Kevlar helmets, and other tactical equipment;
- Officers may be armed with rifles, shotguns, and/or handguns; and
- Officers may shout commands and may push individuals to the ground for their safety.

How to react when law enforcement arrives:

- Try to remain calm;
- Follow officers' instructions;
- Put down any items in your hands (e.g., bags, jackets);
- Immediately raise hands and spread fingers;
- Keep hands visible at all times;
- Avoid making quick movements toward officers such as holding on to them;
- Avoid pointing, screaming, and/or yelling; and
- Do **not** stop to ask officers for help or direction when evacuating, just proceed in the direction from which officers are entering the premises.

Information to provide to law enforcement or 9-1-1 operator:

- Location of the active shooter(s);
- Number of shooters, if more than one;
- Physical description of shooter(s);
- Number and type of weapons held by the shooter(s); and
- Number of potential targets at the location.

The first officers to arrive to the scene will not stop to help injured persons. Expect rescue teams comprised of additional officers and emergency medical personnel to follow the initial officers. These rescue teams will treat and remove any injured persons. They may also call upon able-bodied individuals to assist in removing the wounded from the premises.

Once you have reached a safe location or an assembly point, you will likely be held in that area by law enforcement until the situation is under control, and all witnesses have been identified and questioned. Do not leave until law enforcement authorities have instructed you to do so.

SECTION 5: UNTIL HELP ARRIVES

CERT volunteers are NOT equipped or trained to respond to terrorist incidents. CERT volunteers should in no way activate or respond to an incident in their community.

However, while highly unlikely, it is possible that you may find yourself in a situation that you believe to be a terrorist attack. In this rare circumstance, CERT volunteers have a developed skillset to provide care until help arrives.

Like in any other situation, volunteers should follow the direction of law enforcement and first responders. You should be mindful of your limits and recognize that your safety is your top priority. Stay safe. Do not put yourself at risk but save lives if you can.

If you are willing and able to assist, remember the most important life-saving interventions, recognize what the stress of the situation can do to you, and understand the physical impact of being in a potential terrorist situation.

Treating Others

If you believe you are able to help those around you, focus on the lifesaving interventions that were covered in Unit 3.

- **Stop Bleeding:** The average person has approximately five liters of blood. Severe blood loss can result in irreversible shock. This means that if you lose about half of your body's blood supply, no matter what anyone does to try to save you, death is unavoidable. You must get bleeding under control as soon as possible. The first way to control severe bleeding is through applying direct pressure. For more information on controlling bleeding, please refer to page 3-4 of the Unit 3 Participant Manual.
- **Maintain Body Temperature:** It is important to maintain the patient's body temperature. If necessary, place a blanket or other material under and/or over the patient to provide protection from extreme ground temperatures (hot or cold). People with very serious injuries are more susceptible to hypothermia, which can increase the risk of death. For more information on maintaining body temperature, please refer to page 3-5 of the Unit 3 Participant Manual.
- **Opening the Airway:** Positioning an injured patient to keep their airway open and clear is critical to saving their life. The best position for the body is one in which the chest can expand fully and the airway is not at risk of being obstructed. In other words, the best position is one in which the tongue cannot flop back into the individual's throat and one in which blood or fluid does not end up in the lungs (aspirated), particularly in the case with someone with facial trauma. There are different ways to position an injured patient to keep their airway open depending on if the patient is conscious or unconscious. For more information on opening the airway, please refer to page 3-7 of the Unit 3 Participant Manual.
- **Providing Comfort:** CERT volunteers can be of great value to injured and emotional patient simply by offering comfort and support. No special skills are needed—just a calm and reassuring presence. For more information on providing comfort, please refer to page 3-9 of the Unit 3 Participant Manual.

You must make the best decisions possible with the information that you have at hand. Even if an incident turns out not to be terrorist related, you have made the right decision if you have done the most good for the greatest number and have not been injured.

Recognizing Stress

Before you step forward to help it is important to recognize how the stress of the situation may affect you. In any life-threatening situation, you will feel fear and this fear will impact your mind and body. It is important for you to be aware of what may happen, so you can recognize these responses as a normal part of your body's response to stress. It is normal to experience certain physical and psychological changes. Recognize that:

- Fear is typically at its peak once we comprehend the danger of the situation;
- Fear has profound effects on the mind and body; and
- Fear can influence action.

Physical Impact

Explosions create a high-pressure blast that sends debris flying and lifts people off the ground. The type of injuries and the number of people hurt will vary depending on: the physical environment and the size of the blast, the amount of shielding between people and the blast, fires or structural damage that result from the explosion, and whether the explosion occurs in a closed space or an open area. Injuries common to explosions include:

- Overpressure damage to the lungs, ears, abdomen, and other pressure sensitive organs. Blast lung injury, a condition caused by the extreme pressure of an explosion, is the leading cause of illness and death for initial survivors of an explosion.
- Fragmentation injuries caused by projectiles thrown by the blast—material from the bomb, shrapnel, or flying debris that penetrates the body and causes damage.
- Impact injuries are caused when the blast throws a person into another object causing serious injuries, including fractures, amputation, and trauma to the head and neck.
- Thermal injuries caused by burns to the skin, mouth, sinuses, and lungs.
- Other injuries including exposure to toxic substances, crush injuries, and aggravation of pre-existing conditions (e.g., asthma, congestive heart failure).

Remember life-saving interventions for controlling bleeding, maintaining body temperature, and opening airways that were taught in Unit 3: Disaster Medical Operations Part 1.

Secondary Attacks

Terrorist attacks, especially those involving explosives, may include a secondary wave targeting those who are providing care to the injured. Be highly aware of your surroundings and move away from danger as soon as you are able. If you can do so, take others with you.

A bomb explosion can cause secondary explosions if gasoline, natural gas, or other flammable material is ignited. Secondary hazards that result can include fire with possibly toxic smoke, disruption of electric power, ruptured natural gas lines and water mains, and debris. There can be loss of traffic control in the blast area with possible traffic accidents involving fleeing citizens.

What Professional Responders Will Do

There are several measures that you can expect professional responders to take when they arrive at the scene of a terrorist incident.

Size-up

The first step that professional responders will take when they arrive at the scene is to conduct a thorough size-up. They will follow steps that are very similar to those that CERTs take to determine:

- What is going on;
- How bad the situation is and how much worse it could get;
- What measures can be taken to control the incident safely; and
- What resources will be needed.

Establish Zones

CERTs can expect professional responders to treat some terrorist incidents the same as hazardous materials incidents. As such, the next step that they will take is to establish three incident zones.

1. The **Hot Zone** is referred to as the incident scene and the contaminated area around the scene.
2. The **Warm Zone** in a decontamination situation would be upwind (and upstream if the contaminant is waterborne) from the Hot Zone and is used to isolate survivors during decontamination. In a non-decontamination situation, such as a terrorist attack, the warm zone will be the area immediately outside of the incident scene.
3. The **Cold Zone** is located beyond the Warm Zone. Survivors will be evacuated to the Cold Zone and kept there until professional responders authorize them to leave.

SECTION 6: HAZMAT AND CBRNE

It is highly unlikely that CERT volunteers will find themselves working within a Hazmat or CBRNE incident. However, there are some basic guidelines that can be noted for these types of incidents.

Basic HAZMAT Decontamination Procedures

The objective of decontamination is to remove harmful chemicals or particles of radioactive dirt or dust that have come in contact with the skin or clothes.

- Leave the contaminated area immediately. Depending on the circumstances, go inside, go outside, or go upwind, uphill, or upstream from the contaminant. (Seek a distance of at least 1,000 to 1,500 feet.)
- Take decontamination action. Seconds count! The goal is to limit the time that the agent is in contact with the skin.
  — Remove everything from the body, including jewelry. Cut off clothing that would normally be removed over the head to reduce the probability of inhaling or ingesting the agent. Seal your clothes in a plastic bag.
  — Wash hands before using them to shower. If no shower is available, improvise with water from faucets or bottled water.
  — Flush the entire body, including the eyes, underarms, and groin area, with copious amounts of cool water. Hot water opens the pores of the skin and can promote absorption of the contaminant. Using copious amounts of water is important because some chemicals react to small amounts of water.

If soap is immediately available, mix the soap with water for decontamination. Avoid scrubbing with soap because scrubbing can rub the chemical into the skin rather than remove it.

Wash hair with soap or shampoo or rinse with water if soap is not available. Do not use conditioner as that can bind radioactive materials to your hair and make it difficult to remove.

If hosing someone else off or pouring water from a container, avoid both physical contact with the person and with the runoff.

The water used for decontamination must be contained and covered or drained outside of the shelter area to avoid shelter contamination.

Blot dry using an absorbent cloth. Do not rub the skin! Put on clean clothes.

As soon as possible, emergency responders will set up mass decontamination capabilities. For radiological events, stations for radiation monitoring and blood tests will also be set up to determine levels of exposure and what next steps to take to protect health.

CBRNE

CBRNE stands for chemical, biological, radiological, nuclear, and high-yield explosive. These events have the capability to cause mass casualties and cause great public unrest. The anthrax letter attacks in 2001 are an example of how effective and disrupting a CBRNE attack could be. The threat of CBRNE attacks has become less likely as terrorists have moved on to new tactics, as discussed earlier in this unit.

A CBRNE incident differs from a hazardous material incident in both scope (i.e., CBRNE can be a mass casualty situation) and intent. CBRNE incidents are responded to under the assumption that they are intentional and malicious.

CBRNE Indicators

It is important to be alert to changes in the environment as a clue to a possible terrorist attack.

While bombs and explosions have obvious immediate effects, biological or chemical attacks may not be as immediately noticeable. Indicators that a biological or chemical attack has occurred or is underway could include:

- Vapor clouds or mists that are unusual for the area or for the time of day.
- Out of place and unattended packages, boxes, or vehicles. Items that are out of place and unattended could signal a possible terrorist attack. This could include chemical or biological agents as well as explosives.

If you observe any of these indicators of a terrorist incident, you should:

- Not touch it;
- Move away from the object or area; and
- Report it to authorities immediately.

Nuclear Attack

A nuclear weapon is an explosive device that derives its destructive force from nuclear reaction. All nuclear devices cause deadly effects when exploded, including blinding light, intense heat, initial nuclear radiation, blast, fires started by the heat pulse, secondary fires caused by the destruction, and widespread radioactive material that can contaminate the air, water, and ground surfaces for miles around.

A nuclear device can range from a weapon carried by an intercontinental ballistic missile launched by a hostile nation or terrorist organization, to a small portable nuclear device transported by an individual.

In the very unlikely event you believe you are in a nuclear attack or exposed to radiation, there are three factors that significantly affect your safety after the incident: time, distance, and shielding. A critical protective action in a radiological or nuclear event is to get inside as quickly as possible, stay inside, and stay tuned to local radio or television stations for further guidance.

- **Stay Inside (time):** Limiting the amount of time in the area of an incident is important to limit exposure to radioactive fallout resulting from the explosion. Remain inside until you receive notification from authorities that it is safe to leave the building. In most cases, be prepared to shelter inside for a few days. However, sheltering may be necessary for as long as a month.

- **Go Deep Inside (distance/shielding):** It is important to find adequate shelter quickly to avoid radioactive fallout resulting from the explosion. Get inside as soon as possible and go to the farthest interior room or to a basement. Flat roofs collect fallout particles, so the top floor is not a good choice, nor is a floor adjacent to a neighboring flat roof. The more distance between you and the fallout particles, the better.

If you are outside when the event occurs, do not look at the flash or fire ball. It can blind you. Take cover behind anything that will offer protection, lie flat, and cover your head. If the explosion is some distance away, it could take 30 seconds or more for the blast wave to hit. Get inside as soon as you can.

Shelter-in-Place

You may receive direction from law enforcement to shelter-in-place. Depending on the nature of the threat (if it is chemical or biological), this may involve sealing yourself into a room. Procedures for sheltering in place during a chemical or biological attack include:

- Shut off the ventilation system and latch all doors and windows to reduce airflow from the outside.
- Go to your shelter-in-place room (where your precut plastic, duct tape, radio, and other supplies should be stored).
- Use precut plastic sheeting to cover openings where air can enter the room, including doors, windows, vents, electrical outlets, and telephone outlets. When cut, the sheeting should extend several inches beyond the dimensions of the door or window to allow room to duct tape the sheeting to the walls and floor.
- Tape the plastic sheeting around all doors and windows using duct tape to ensure a good seal.
- Seal with duct tape other areas where air can come in, such as under doors and areas where pipes enter the home. Air can be blocked by placing towels or other soft objects in areas where air could enter, then securing them with duct tape.
- Chemicals used in an attack will be carried on the wind and will dissipate over time. You will generally not need to stay in a sealed room for more than a few hours. Monitor Emergency Alert System broadcasts to know when it is safe to leave the safe room.
- After contaminants have cleared, open windows and vents and turn on fans to provide ventilation.

To be able to execute these procedures during an actual event, requires that you:

- Store precut plastic sheeting in your identified shelter-in-place room.
- Assemble and store food, water, and a battery-operated radio in the shelter-in-place room.
- Practice sealing the room.
- Establish shelter-in-place procedures wherever you spend significant amounts of time at home, at work, and/or at school.

As a rule of thumb, 10 square feet of floor space per person will provide sufficient air to prevent carbon dioxide buildup for up to 5 hours, assuming a normal breathing rate while resting.

If the threat is a violent individual(s), shelter-in-place may be referred to as a lockout and you may be asked to lock yourself into a safe space by doing the following:

- Lock exterior doors.
- Clear hallways, restrooms, and other rooms that cannot be secured.
- Move all persons away from windows. Secure and cover windows, if able.
- Make only essential communications and avoid any broadcasts about the movement, location, or status of law enforcement in the area.
- Once the threat has subsided, law enforcement announces, "all clear" and operations can return to normal.

UNIT 8 SUMMARY

The key points from this unit are:

- The definition of terrorism, as defined by the Department of Justice, is the "unlawful use of force or violence against persons or property to intimidate or coerce a government, the civilian population, or any segment thereof, in furtherance of political or social objectives." Terrorism may be perpetrated by foreign or domestic individuals or groups.
- When terrorists attack, their goals are to:
    - Create mass casualties;
    - Disrupt critical resources, vital services, and the economy; and
    - Cause fear.
- Terrorists have moved away from large, resource-intensive plots to complex, coordinated attacks like those in Paris, France in 2016.
- New tactics include active shooter events and detonating improvised explosive devices, sometimes occurring simultaneously in coordinated attacks. In addition, an evolving terrorist tactic is cyberterrorism.
- An Active Shooter is an individual actively engaged in killing or attempting to kill people in a confined and populated area; in most cases, active shooters use firearms(s) and there is no pattern or method to their selection of targets. Active shooter situations are unpredictable and evolve quickly. Typically, the immediate deployment of law enforcement is required to stop the shooting and mitigate harm to survivors.
- Run, Hide, Fight is the best way to respond if an active shooter is in your vicinity.
- An IED attack is the use of a "homemade" bomb and/or destructive device to destroy, incapacitate, harass, or distract. Because they are improvised, IEDs can come in many forms, ranging from a small pipe bomb to a sophisticated device capable of causing massive damage and loss of life.
- CERT volunteers, along with the public, play a critical role in identifying suspicious activities occurring within the community. There are typically eight signs of terrorism that signal potential terrorist activity. If identified and communicated correctly to local law enforcement, suspicious activities surrounding the potential possibility of a terrorist attack can be stopped. The eight signs of terrorism are:

    - Surveillance;
    - Elicitation;
    - Tests of security;
    - Funding;
    - Acquiring supplies;
    - Impersonation or suspicious people who don't belong;
    - Rehearsal and dry runs; and
    - Deployment.
- Terrorist attacks frequently occur without warning; however, being alert, reporting suspicious activities, and taking general preparedness steps, such as having a plan to communicate with loved ones, will help you if one does occur. If you

believe a terrorist attack is imminent, call 9-1-1 and follow the instructions provided.

- CERT volunteers are NOT equipped or trained to response to terrorist incidents. CERT volunteers should in no way activate or respond to an incident in their community.
- While highly unlikely, it is possible that you may find yourself in a situation that you believe is a terrorist attack. Like in any other situation, be mindful of your limits and recognize that your safety is your top priority. Stay safe. Do not put yourself at risk but save lives if you can.
- It is important to be alert to changes in the environment as a clue to possible CBRNE attack.
  - Vapor clouds or mists that are unusual for the area or for the time of day.
  - Out of place and unattended packages, boxes, or vehicles. Items that are out of place and unattended could signal a possible terrorist attack. This could include chemical or biological agents as well as explosives.
- If you observe any of these indicators:
  - Do **not** touch it;
  - Move away from the area; and
  - Report it to authorities immediately.

Homework Assignment

Review the materials to be presented in the next session.

CERT Unit 9: Course Review, Final Exam, and Disaster Simulation

Participant Manual

CERT Unit 9: Course Review, Final Exam and Disaster Simulation

This unit includes:

- ☐ **A Review of Key Points from the Course**
- ☐ **A Final Exam**
- ☐ **A Final Exercise**

CERT Unit 9 Table of Contents

SECTION 1: COURSE REVIEW

Course Overview

If you do not remember a particular key point, refer back to that specific unit.

Unit 1: Disaster Preparedness

- Home and workplace preparedness
  - Assembling a disaster supply kit
  - Developing a disaster plan
  - Developing a safe room
  - Evacuation versus sheltering-in-place
- Specific preparedness measures for local high-risk hazards (including terrorism)

Unit 2: CERT Organization

- Organizational structure
  - Well-defined management structure
  - Effective communications among agency personnel
  - Accountability
- Command objectives
  - Identify the scope of the incident through damage assessment
  - Determine an overall strategy and logistical requirements
  - Deploy resources efficiently but safely

Units 3 and 4: Disaster Medical Operations

- Life-threatening conditions
- Methods for controlling bleeding
  - Direct pressure
  - Tourniquets
  - Recognizing shock
- Maintaining body temperature
- Opening the airway
  - Positioning
  - Jaw-thrust maneuver
- Wound care
- Special considerations when head, neck, or spinal injuries are suspected
- Treatment area considerations
- Splinting and bandaging
- Basic treatment for various injuries
- Establishing a treatment area
- Head-to-toe assessments

Unit 5: Disaster Psychology

- In the aftermath of disasters, survivors and disaster workers can experience psychological and physiological symptoms of stress

- The steps CERT leaders should take to reduce stress on team members
- The steps CERT members can take to reduce their own stress levels
- Strategies for helping survivors work through their trauma

Unit 6: Fire Safety and Utility Controls

- Fire chemistry
  - The fire triangle
  - Classes of fire
- Fire size-up considerations: size-up of a situation involving a fire and the additional fire considerations
- Firefighting resources
  - General resources available
  - Portable fire extinguishers, their capabilities and limitations
- Fire suppression safety
  - Safety equipment must be used at all times
  - CERT members must always use the buddy system
  - Fire suppression group leaders should always have a backup team available
- Fire and utility hazards
  - Electrical
  - Natural gas
  - Flammable liquids
- Hazardous materials
  - Identification
  - Defensive strategies

Unit 7: Light Search and Rescue

- Search and rescue are really two functions
- Goals of search and rescue
  - Rescuing the greatest number of people in the shortest amount of time
  - Rescuing the lightly trapped survivors first
- Size-up
  - Construction types
  - Related hazards
- Structural damage
  - Light damage
  - Moderate damage
  - Heavy damage
- Search techniques
  - Be systematic and thorough
  - Mark areas searched
  - Document search results
- Rescue techniques
  - Survivor carries
  - Leverage and cribbing

— Lifts and drags

Unit 8: Terrorism

- Active shooter tactics
- CBRNE indicators
- CERT protocols for terrorist incidents
- Protective actions following a terrorist incident

SECTION 2: CERT BASIC TRAINING FINAL EXAM

Unit 1: Disaster Preparedness

1. When a disaster occurs, a CERT member's first responsibility is to:
    A. Join the CERT in disaster response efforts
    B. Help professional responders
    C. Ensure personal and family safety
    D. Do the greatest good for the greatest number of people

2. CERT members volunteer to fill non-disaster roles. An example of a non-disaster function of CERTs is:
    A. Staffing parades, health fairs, and other special events
    B. Monitoring the news for potential disaster threats
    C. Petitioning local officials for more local emergency response funding
    D. Distributing political pamphlets and other materials

3. There are five types of disasters. They are natural, terrorist, home fires, pandemic and _____.
    A. Mechanical
    B. Biological
    C. Chemical
    D. Technological and Accidental

4. Which of the following is NOT a hazard associated with home fixtures?
    A. Gas line ruptures
    B. Hazardous material spill
    C. Injury or electric shock
    D. Fire from faulty wiring

5. One of the steps in preparing for a disaster is to develop a disaster supply kit. Where should you keep separate disaster supply kits?
    A. Home and work
    B. Every room in the house
    C. Vehicle
    D. Home, work, and vehicle

Unit 2: CERT Organization

Following an earthquake, you and your fellow CERT members mobilize and meet at a disaster scene, where fire and law enforcement officials have already arrived. Before taking action, you work with the professional responders to get organized.

1. What is the name of the system used by emergency response agencies to manage emergency responses?
   A. Incident Command System (ICS)
   B. Strategic Planning Unit (SPU)
   C. Search and Rescue System (SRS)
   D. Rescue Command System (RCS)

2. In the CERT command structure, how is the CERT leader established?
   A. By being the first person to arrive on the scene
   B. By seniority
   C. By department
   D. By the local police chief

You are the CERT Team Leader and therefore responsible for directing team activities. You establish a Command Post for your CERT.

3. What should you do if you have to leave the command post for whatever reason?
   A. Ask a law enforcement official to take over while you're gone
   B. Designate CERT Team Leader status to someone else in the Command Post
   C. Leave without delegating any of your Team Leader responsibilities
   D. You may never leave the Command Post under any circumstances

4. CERT members should always be assigned to teams of at least how many people?
   A. Six
   B. Three
   C. Two
   D. Four

5. A woman comes up to a disaster scene that you have determined is unsafe to enter. What should you do?
   A. Warn her that the situation is unsafe
   B. Threaten to call the police if she attempts to enter
   C. Physically restrain her from entering
   D. Nothing; you should let her be

6. To whom should you give documentation?
   A. The first professional responders on the scene
   B. Your local CERT leader
   C. Keep it for your own records
   D. The National CERT Program Office

7. Which of the following forms contains essential information for tracking the overall situation?
    A. Survivor Treatment Area Record
    B. CERT Assignment Tracking Log
    C. Message form
    D. Equipment Resources form

Unit 3: Disaster Medical Operations — Part 1

In the aftermath of a magnitude 7.7 earthquake, you have ensured your safety and your family's safety, and you grab your CERT kit and PPE. As you are making your way to your CERT's established meeting point, you come across a woman lying by the side of the road. You call out your name and affiliation and ask, "Are you okay?" There is no response.

1. Based on what you know thus far, how should you proceed?
    A. Assume the woman is dead and continue to the CERT meeting point
    B. Call 9-1-1 on your cell phone immediately
    C. Assess for airway obstruction, excessive bleeding, and low body temperature
    D. Make a note of the woman's location and go for help

You move closer to the survivor. Once again, you ask, "Can you hear me? Are you okay?" As you approach, you hear a very faint "help me," and now that you are closer, you notice that that the survivor is bleeding heavily from a wound on her thigh. You immediately attempt to call 9-1-1 on you cell phone but the system is down.

2. You know this woman is seriously injured. How would you help her?
    A. Assess for life-threatening conditions systematically, starting with the airway
    B. Focus immediately on the most critical threat, the heavy bleeding
    C. Get blankets from your supply kit because this woman is clearly in shock
    D. Keep the woman company until more help arrives

3. You notice that the blood is spurting from the wound on the survivor's inner thigh. What type of bleeding is this?
    A. Arterial
    B. Venous
    C. Capillary
    D. Mortal

4. What is the first thing you do to stop the bleeding?
    A. Apply a tourniquet
    B. Wrap the wound with the first piece of cloth you can find
    C. Elevate the survivor's heart above the wound by having the woman sit up
    D. Using the sterile dressings in your supply kit, apply pressure directly to the wound

After a few moments, the bleeding slows considerably. You ask the woman, "Are you okay? Squeeze my hand if you can hear me." She is only able to groan unintelligibly in response. You notice that her fingers are cold — despite soaring temperatures — when she tries to squeeze your hand.

5. The signs and symptoms that you witness tell you that this woman is suffering from what?
   A. Low blood sugar
   B. Shock due to inadequate blood flow
   C. Malnourishment
   D. Shock due to the extreme stress of the situation

6. How would you treat the woman based on your findings?
   A. Wrap her in something warm
   B. Tell her to go to sleep
   C. Ask her to hold the dressing in place while you search for help
   D. Give her food and water

You arrive at the meeting point and your CERT Team Leader assigns you to help with the survivors. A woman runs into the treatment area holding a little boy and frantically calling out, "Someone please help my son, he's turning blue! I don't think he can breathe!" You turn and run to help the woman. You ask her to put her son down so you can help.

7. What is the first thing that you should do?
   A. Conduct a head-to-toe assessment
   B. Have another volunteer lead the mother away
   C. Assess for airway, bleeding, and low body temperature
   D. Perform CPR

While listening for lung sounds, you notice that the boy is wheezing and his lips are blue. You cannot find anything obvious obstructing his airway. As you glance down quickly at the rest of the boy's body, you notice an angry red welt on his inner arm.

8. You have reason to suspect that this boy is suffering from:
   A. Anaphylaxis
   B. An unknown blood-borne disease
   C. Hypertension
   D. Hypothermia

Unit 4: Disaster Medical Operations — Part 2

A Category 4 hurricane has just struck your town. You are assigned by your Team Leader to the treatment area. You are directed to help with the survivors. A fellow team member asks you to get some clean water to wash soiled gloves. You know the supply team is on its way but could be several hours away. Grabbing a bucket, you run to a nearby stream for water.

1. What should you do to sterilize the water for medical use?
   A. Mix 1-part bleach and 10 parts water
   B. Mix in 8 drops of non-perfumed chlorine bleach per gallon of water and wait for 30 minutes
   C. Take the bucket and find a place to boil the water, since you assume that one of the buildings must have a functional kitchen
   D. Mix in 8 tablespoons of non-perfumed chlorine bleach and wait for 30 seconds

Once you arrive back at the treatment area with the water, the team leader explains that a survivor has died. The team leader puts you in charge of establishing the morgue.

2. How and where will you set up the morgue?
   A. Near the treatment area
   B. Inside the treatment area
   C. Away from the treatment areas
   D. None of the above

A few hours later, you return to the treatment area and ask your Team Leader for a new assignment. She quickly explains that the area is overflowing with survivors and asks you to help perform rapid head-to-toe assessments.

3. What acronym does the medical community use to remember what to look for when conducting a rapid assessment?
   A. DCAP-PMS
   B. SALT
   C. DCAP-BTLS
   D. IDMD-SALT

While performing your first assessment on a young adult male, you notice bruising around the eyes and blood in the nose. The survivor says his hands feel numb and he is unable to move them.

4. While it is impossible to be sure out in the field, you should assume that:
   A. The survivor is in shock
   B. The survivor will die unless you find a medical professional
   C. The survivor is bleeding internally
   D. The survivor has a closed-head, neck, or spinal injury

Unit 5: Disaster Psychology

You and your fellow CERT members arrive at a neighboring community following a devastating tornado. Survivors have been sifting through debris and have found six bodies. They tell you about what it was like to find the bodies. One of your fellow CERT members starts feeling nauseated. He is obviously overwhelmed.

1. Which of the following is not an example of a physiological symptom of trauma?
     A. Hyperactivity
     B. Denial
     C. Headaches
     D. Loss of appetite

Some of the survivors you rescue exhibit signs of trauma, and you've warned your team ahead of time that they should expect some of the psychological effects will be directed toward them. In order to help your team better understand what the survivors are going through, you've also explained the six phases of a crisis following a disaster.

2. During which phase do survivors attempt to assess the damage and locate other survivors?
     A. Pre-disaster phase
     B. Impact phase
     C. Honeymoon phase
     D. Heroic phase

The goal of on-scene psychological intervention by CERT members is to stabilize the incident scene by stabilizing individuals. You come across a man who is in shock and bleeding from his chest.

3. What should you do first?
     A. Listen empathetically
     B. Attempt to locate the man's family or friends to provide natural support
     C. Say, "You'll get through this"
     D. Address the man's medical needs

4. Which of the following is not a step that your team's members should take in the future to personally reduce stress?
     A. Eat a balanced diet
     B. Get enough sleep
     C. Take antidepressants
     D. Connect with others

Unit 6: Fire Safety and Utility Controls

While searching a lightly damaged structure following a destructive storm, you and fellow CERT members locate a fire.

1. As you conduct your fire size-up, which of the following is the least important question to consider:
   A. Can my buddy and I fight the fire safely?
   B. Do my buddy and I have the right equipment?
   C. How many people are in the building?
   D. Can my buddy and I escape?

From your size-up, you determine that the fire can be put out with a portable fire extinguisher. You and your buddy quickly retrieve a portable fire extinguisher, which you have determined is the right type of extinguisher to fight this fire.

2. What should you do before approaching the fire?
   A. Test the extinguisher after pulling the pin
   B. Wait for the fire department to arrive
   C. Tell your buddy to wait at the door for you
   D. Make sure the house's water supply is shut off

Following the correct CERT procedure (P.A.S.S.), you discharge the extinguisher.

3. What should you do if the fire continues to burn 5 seconds after you start to extinguish it?
   A. Check the label on the extinguisher
   B. Look for creative resources to fight the fire
   C. Leave immediately
   D. Back out and signal for your buddy to attempt to suppress the fire

4. The fire has spread to other areas by the time the fire department arrives. What's your next course of action?
   A. Attempt to suppress the fire again with a new extinguisher
   B. Communicate what you know to one of the firefighters
   C. Overhaul the fire
   D. Send in a backup team to fight the fire

5. If the chief officer asks you and your fellow CERT members to remain outside at a safe distance, how should you respond?
   A. Continue to conduct a size-up from a safe distance outside of the building
   B. Leave the premises
   C. Enter the house after the firefighters
   D. Call in more CERT members for backup

While the fire department manages to suppress most of the fire inside the building, a small fire has started to spread through the yard. You notice a nearby shed is posted with an NFPA 704 Diamond featuring the numbers 1, 1, and 2.

6. What should you do?

      A. Suppress and overhaul the fire because the numbers in the Diamond are small and indicate that little risk is present

      B. Leave the area and communicate the information to one of the professional firefighters on the scene if they are accessible

      C. Suppress and overhaul the fire only if the number in the blue quadrant is less than 2

      D. Make sure you are using the correct type of fire extinguisher

Unit 7: Light Search and Rescue Operations

After a tornado ravages a nearby community, you and your fellow CERT members volunteer to help with the search and rescue operations. You arrive on the scene to discover collapsed houses, cars swept up into trees, and various debris strewn everywhere.

1. As you begin the CERT size-up process, what is the first thing you should do?
   - A. Gather facts
   - B. Assess and communicate damage
   - C. Establish priorities
   - D. Consider probabilities

You and three other CERT members begin searching the local library, a large brick building where many people in the community were instructed to take cover before the storm. A size-up of the building reveals superficial damage, including broken windows and cracked plaster.

2. How would you classify the damage to the building?
   - A. Heavy damage
   - B. Moderate damage
   - C. Light damage
   - D. Slight damage

As you continue your search of the library, you make a single slash next to the doorway of the first room you enter.

3. What information do you write in what will become the left quadrant of this search marking?
   - A. Information about hazards and collapses
   - B. The number of survivors in the room
   - C. Your agency or group ID
   - D. The room number

While stopping frequently to listen, you hear a faint cry for help from the corner of the room. You walk over to find a young boy who has glass shards in his leg and is unable to walk.

4. Keeping in mind that you are searching the room with only two other CERT members, which of the following is not a recommended way of moving the boy?
   - A. Blanket carry
   - B. Pack-strap carry
   - C. Chair carry
   - D. One-person arm carry

Upon completing your search and rescue in the library, you enter a house where the second floor has collapsed, creating a lean-to void.

5. How should you proceed?
   A. Leave the premises immediately and mark the structure as unsound
   B. Quickly search the ground floor
   C. Use an axe or similar tool to knock down the floor and clear the void
   D. Call for backup

Unit 8: Terrorism and CERT

You are having a business lunch downtown when you hear a loud explosion. You follow others outside to find what caused the noise. In the distance you can see heavy smoke rising from the electrical plant, the very same electrical plant used to power your town and several major cities in the area and that you saw on the news last night cited as a potential target for a recently uncovered terrorist plot. All around you, people are speculating that the plot was successful.

1. What is the first thing you should do?
    A. Gather your CERT equipment and report for duty
    B. Locate your family and evacuate to safety
    C. Call the Federal Government to alert it about a terrorist attack
    D. Initially monitor the situation from a safe place

You remember from the news report that the potential plot was uncovered when an electrical plant security guard noticed the same black van parked outside for over a week. Worried that someone was watching the building, he alerted local authorities.

2. Which of the eight signs of a terrorist attack did the security guard notice?
    A. Surveillance
    B. Tests of security
    C. Acquiring supplies
    D. Dry runs

A friend runs over to you, a little frantic, and asks why you are not headed to the disaster site to help. After all, he says, you are a trained CERT member.

3. How do you respond to your friend?
    A. "Yes. You're right. I'm heading in that direction now."
    B. "I am a CERT member, but I have to wait for an official to declare a disaster before I can activate."
    C. "I'm not part of the Terrorist Response Team."
    D. "You're right. I am a CERT member, but CERT members must not respond to a potential terrorist incident."

SECTION 3: DISASTER SIMULATION

Purpose: This simulation will give you a chance to apply many of the skills you learned during the earlier sessions.

Instructions:

1. Break into four groups.
2. The simulation will be conducted across four stations.
3. At Station 1, each group will receive the disaster simulation. Based on that scenario, you will:
    - Determine the extent of damage
    - Establish team priorities
    - Determine the resources needed
    - Identify potential hazards
4. While at Station 1, your group will select a CERT Team Leader who will establish a CERT organization based on resources available and establish priorities.
5. At Station 2, your group will be required to:
    - Evaluate a fire situation
    - Select the proper extinguisher for the situation
    - Extinguish the fire

Each person will be required to extinguish the fire.

6. At Station 3, your group will be required to treat survivors with the medical supplies available.
7. At Station 4, your group will perform leveraging and cribbing to extricate survivors who are trapped by debris.
8. Your group will have approximately 15 minutes at each station.

Image 9.1: Disaster Simulation Map

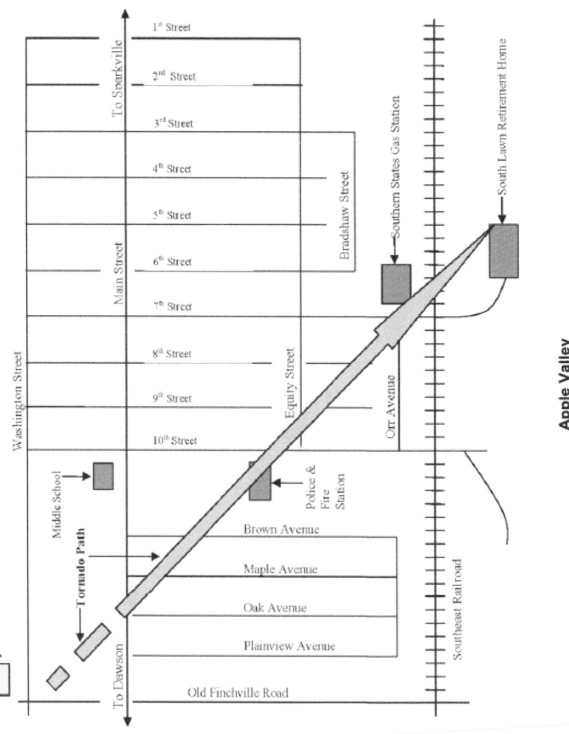

SECTION 4: COURSE CONCLUSION

Don't forget the importance of continuing education and training to maintain and improve your skills and knowledge. You can attend:

- Periodic refresher training that is offered locally;
- Standard and advanced first aid courses that are offered through organizations such as the American Red Cross;
- Cardiopulmonary resuscitation (CPR) classes that are offered through organizations such as the American Red Cross or the American Heart Association; and
- Independent Study (IS) courses available online from FEMA at www.training.fema.gov/IS/.

Made in the USA
Middletown, DE
12 August 2024

58973476R00150